*For the child in all of
dream at the water's edge . . .*

Contents

Acknowledgements

I would like to gratefully acknowledge two people in my life, without whose input this book would not exist. First, I want to thank my mom, Michelle Labbat Shulman, for inspiring me to never give up and always strive to overcome all the obstacles that can hold us back. Her journey has been a source of constant and profound inspiration to me and her words of encouraging wisdom are indelibly etched in my spirit. She taught me that so long as I have a voice, I would be fine in the world. The combination of perseverance and ability to ask questions she instilled in me has led to this water discovery, which has unlocked my passion and talent.

Thank you, Mom.

The second person I would like to thank is my dear friend, writer and editor Eric Herman. He was the only person who listened to me 10 years ago about my water quality ranting and in the time since we've worked together exploring and refining our shared vision for the industry. His keen listening ability and extreme talent for wordsmithing has made this book a reality and a work of art.

For that I thank you, Sensei.

The journey is its own reward.

The author at sea

Introduction

Let's begin with a provocative question – have swimming pools become obsolete?

That might seem surprising coming from someone who earns his living in the pool, spa, and aquatics industry, and it's a question I've never heard from any other professional in the business, or from a consumer for that matter. Yet, I think it's something worth considering as we look to the future of the aquatic experience and where we stand today.

So, are pools, in reality, becoming obsolete, are they a feature more of the past than the future? That question leads to a surprisingly complex set of issues in which the answers are both more subtle and profound than one might initially suspect.

In terms of obsolescence on the most literal level, we know that a great many pools, especially those that serve the general public, have old worn-out equipment and dodgy designs that have become dated and need replacing. Upgrading equipment and/or aesthetic features can be quite expensive and as a result many resource-strapped facilities and property owners are forced to keep their old and inadequate systems operating for as long as possible — and never mind the drab appearance.

But that's really only a small part of the answer to the question of obsolescence. There's a much broader context ahead of the inevitability of outdated facilities that I believe is far more important to consider. I'm talking about the social relevance and economic sustainability of pools, as those concepts apply to commercial and public facilities, but also in the residential market as well.

Troubling Narratives

Every year as summer rolls along there's a familiar litany of troublesome public discussions that accompany the swimming season, storylines that point to significant pitfalls and even tragedy in the world of man-made bodies of water. For example, the media annually cycles through echoed reports about infectious contamination in pool and spa water, how consumers should be wary of possible diseases they and their children could contract from being in water containing a host of infectious pathogens with horrible sounding names. We hear about traces of urine and feces in water, as well as respiratory and skin ailments that can go along with human and environmental contamination.

As disturbing as those reports may be, they shrink by comparison to the tragedy of child drowning and the hazards of being in or around the water, another subject that dominates the news at the onset of every swimming season. It's the most difficult topic for the entire aquatics industry, a brutal challenge we all must do a better job of addressing and solving, no question.

Those narratives unfortunately are part of the reason it's not terribly surprising that each year there are more and more reports of public pools closing, almost always for lack of funding, and there are also the stories about consumers filling in their backyard pools. Now, I'm not a negative person by nature, far from it, but I do think it's critical for our industry to look at these challenges in order to identify and implement practical solutions. That means facing tough questions.

So, do all of those negatives add up to the stark realization that pools have, indeed, become obsolete? I believe the answer is both yes and no.

Obviously, the state of the aquatics industry is far from where it should be and the future is uncertain, if not gloomy in some respects. If we mean to thrive as a viable part of the recreational economy now and in the future, we have to up our game, which is the primary subject of this book.

That's why I'm so passionate about the advent of the water quality professional, which I see as one of the most important evolutionary steps we must take to change with the times. In terms of technology and methodology, we can embrace a far more scientific and data-driven approach to water quality management, and we should promote more systematic procedures for everything from initial design to how daily maintenance unfolds.

In many ways, our future will be defined by our ability to

embrace a far more technically disciplined way of engineering and managing all aspects of water quality and the overall environment. That's why we need to develop the professional category of the water quality manager.

Enduring Relevance

For all of the challenges and potential solutions we face going forward, it's also equally critical that we embrace the positive side of the discussion. In many very, very important ways, pools will never be obsolete. On the most fundamental level, the desire for the aquatic experience is no different in human beings now than it has been since the dawn of time. People will always want to cool off when it's hot, and swimming will always be the best and most enjoyable way to stay fit. Kids of all ages will always want to splash and play in water. Aquatic spaces will always be among the best venues to share time with family and friends, and for reasons that will never be fully defined by science we will always be drawn to water.

All that dreamy stuff may be highly emotional in nature and nearly impossible to quantify, but it's also the most practical aspect of the aquatics profession. The subjective nature of our relationship with water is precisely why the pool and spa industry exists in the first place. The aquatic experience will never become obsolete because it's hardwired in the human psyche. As professionals, our objective should be to deliver those timeless experiences by providing environments that are as safe and well maintained as humanly possible.

It's the classic yin and yang, the sense and sensibility, the hard science and technology exist entirely to support the sensitive human experience. In man-made environments that contain recreational water, you cannot have the experience without the technical mastery, while at the exact same time all the know-how and ingenuity in the world is useless without the joy and happiness the experience brings.

By overcoming issues of waterborne diseases and bather safety, while increasing convenience, as well as reducing downtime and supporting energy efficiency, we remove the primary obstacles to a positive consumer experience. When the right technology and system engineering is applied in a well-run facility, there's a beautiful dance between science and art. Put another way, a "smart" pool is also a "happy" pool.

Certainly we should also embrace the evolution in consumer expectations that have occurred in recent years. Make no mistake, we do see many pools that feature stunning aesthetic designs, which are often grand expressions of the modern world, and some are downright futuristic. Modern waterparks, for example, push the envelope in terms of interactive designs and fountain technology and give us a universe of visual spectacles. As well, many residential aquatic spaces rival the most luxurious resorts. It's amazing what happens when the imagination is unlocked by technical skill and achievement.

To return to the original question, are pools obsolete?

They certainly don't have to be and that's what this journey is all about.

Meeting the Future

Discover the secret of water

My daughter, Georgia, likes to sum up my career by saying, "My dad was a chef and then he met water."

It's an entirely accurate summation. Yes, I started my professional life as a chef, trained in the fine art of preparing French cuisine. But then I "met water" and became a professional in the aquatics industry, building and maintaining beautiful bodies of water, mostly pools and spas and other water features, as well. Like the fine foods I used to prepare, the water our company provides via both building and service is, by my reckoning, a work of art. It is to borrow the term "gourmet."

The main reason I "found" water as a profession, however, long predates any vocational interest. I was raised on Long Island, New York, on the east side of the island in an area that is largely defined by the oceanic waters that surround it. It's a corner of society that draws its character, culture, and *joie de vivre* from the water. Like many in these parts, and other places with similar fluid fixations, I grew up a child of the aquatic experience.

For as long as I can remember, back to when my parents first took me to the beach at age three, I've been captivated by the ocean and how it always overloads my senses and catapults my spirit. The shimmer of the sunlight on the sparking surface, the sound of the surf, the smell of the spray, and the sensation of buoyancy, all of it is permanently embossed in my brain and my spirit. Later on, as a teen and then as an adult, I embraced sailing as a way to connect with the water. Never have I felt more carefree and joyful than those long treks across the waters of this beautiful region and other places as well. It's always been my happiest of places.

Emotional Impact

I realize all of that has been said countless times by others over the ages, but there's a reason why so many people feel the same way. Water really and truly does have the deepest and most profound impact on our emotions. There's no denying it. While the mechanism of that effect is tough to define exactly, we know it's real because of the way we mark time by the water. It creates memories and psychological bonds you can't find anyplace else.

Truth be told, water holds the only real magic I know of, or at least have directly experienced. Is it that our bodies are comprised of two-thirds water or that over 70 percent of the earth's surface is covered in water? Or is it that we need water to survive or that aquatic environments are alien to us, forbidding and even dangerous? Or is it that we gestate in a fluid environment before we're born? It's probably all of those things to some degree, but whatever the pathology, our fascination with water is an essential component of the human experience. It certainly has been for me.

Now, as I spend my days as the "chef who met water," I've come to know and appreciate it on an entirely different, in some ways, more intimate level. The technical disciplines alone are enough to encompass an entire lifetime of learning. Then there's the joy of creating bodies of water in people's homes and communities that provides them with the excitement and fun that has been with me since childhood.

I realize this is all very idealistic and I don't mean to undersell the many practical challenges of an aquatic career. Like any other worthwhile pursuit, working in this field can be brutally difficult, frustrating, and even at times seemingly unrewarding. Still, this is a vocation that is directly tethered to the nascent aquatic experiences so many of us share and cherish. Ultimately, it's about making people happy! That's why, despite the challenges, I never feel far removed from the joy of meeting water for the very first time.

Water Quality and the Culinary Arts

Of course, I acknowledge that my comparison, some might call it an obsession, between water and fine cuisine might sound surprising even humorous to some, but I've long seen a direct connection between the two professions. When you look into what preparing great food and providing superior water quality are all about, some powerful parallels emerge.

Let me back up: For many years in the late fifties, sixties, and into the seventies, my grandparents, Marieanne and Eugene Labbat, owned and operated the East Hampton restaurant Chez Labbat. During that tenure, Chez Labbat became an extremely well-known local favorite. Jackson Pollock was a regular as were many other celebrities, but you didn't have to be a big shot to feel special there.

As the name suggests, they served French cuisine and they put their hearts and souls into every dish. My grandparents always took an artisan approach to both the food and the way they treated their customers. They focused on every aspect of the dining experience and developed a remarkably loyal following as a result. It was a place where people from all walks of life went to enjoy fabulous meals in an uplifting atmosphere.

Chez Labbat, Long Island

From my kid's eye view, I was heavily influenced by the loving care my grandparents put into their business, which translated into success, both financially and in their stellar reputation. They embraced it all with hard work, joy and passion, and despite many challenges, that effort paid off.

As a direct result of their example, I went on to graduate from the Culinary Institute of Hyde Park in 1987 and later became a sous-chef working at a place called Sardi's in New York City.

Crossing Over

For reasons that are both boring and irrelevant to this discussion, in 1989 I switched careers and started working with my dad, Steven R. Kenny, in his swimming pool service business. Even at the start when I had little to no idea what I was doing, I couldn't help but see the connections between the culinary arts and pool service. Sound strange?

Consider that both fine dining and aquatics provide highly personal experiences that directly relate to health as well as pleasure. Swimming in fetid water and eating unwholesome food are both really bad for you and unpleasant, while healthy eating and swimming in what I sometimes call "gourmet water" are extremely physically beneficial and enjoyable. To my mind, an aquatics facility that has nasty water is not all so different from a restaurant that serves lousy food, and the exact opposite is true. Great food and great water will keep customers coming back because both make them happy and both have real value.

Similarly, a clean aquatics facility that features a comfortable environment around the water, one that doesn't smell bad, for example, is much like a clean and well-appointed dining space. In both cases, the environment supports the core experiences of dining or swimming.

Also, in both professions, chefs and water quality professionals rely on recipes. Great water requires proper mineral balance, sanitization, oxidation, filtration, and circulation. There is, essentially, a cookbook for providing safe and appealing water. (Is it any wonder that health departments regulate both types of businesses?)

Finally, there is a culture of personal service. When I take care of my clients' water, I often think of my grandparents and how they made seamless service their primary business principle.

Similar Missions

When we polish water and tend to the needs of our customers to the finest detail, we're doing the same thing as great restaurateurs; we're creating an experience that consumers will want to revisit over and over again, something they look forward to and may even come to cherish.

So, yes, I do indeed see many direct parallels to fine dining and the aquatic experience. They both have the capacity to make people happy and it's up to us as professionals to make satisfaction job number one – just like my grandparents did all those years ago.

Michelle Labbat Shulman, my mom; Lisa Kenny Bass, my sister; and Marieanne Labbat, my grandmother.

How Water Saved My Life

When you're as passionate as I am about water quality and, indeed, all things aquatic, it's natural that some other people might wonder what motivates such an all-encompassing level of interest. It's a valid question: why is water and its proper care such a huge deal for me?

As I'd imagine is true of many forms of intellectual and emotional obsession, mine starts with personal experience. For a couple of important reasons, my own relationship with water has, at times, transformed my life. As described in the previous pages, circumstances have led me to the water's edge and into the water time and time again, and the aggregate impact on my life has been nearly miraculous.

In the far background are the kinds of experiences that many, if not most, people share. To this day, I can simply sit next to an expanse of water and feel moved by the tranquility and beauty. Small streams and ponds or natural springs also impact my emotions in a very similar way. Not surprising, as an adult sailing is my favorite recreational activity.

Beyond the Shore

If that was all there was to it, that human attraction to water, it would probably be enough to drive my deep involvement.

In my case, however, there's another layer. For several years, I suffered with a litany of serious ailments and symptoms that stumped my doctors. I had pain in my heart, lungs, and throughout my body. I had shortness of breath at times and a chronic lack of energy. I went through every test imaginable and was eventually given the diagnosis that I was reacting to micro-toxins from black mold in my home. It's a common problem that impacts countless people, who like me are very sensitive to the poisons black mold produces.

Long story short, we remediated the mold in our home and I removed myself from the exposure, but I was still very, very sick. I had nowhere to turn until I found a wonderful book titled *My Water Cure* by Sebastian Kneipp, a Bavarian priest who was one of the forefathers of the naturopathic medicine movement. In it, he describes the "Kneipp Cure," which is a form of hydrotherapy that involves the application of water through various methods, temperatures and pressures, all of which he claimed to have therapeutic effects.

Kneipp certainly had his critics and even though I didn't completely understand how it all worked, I also didn't see any harm in giving it a try. I had been working in aquatic service and construction for years at that point and thought to myself, let's see if this H_2O stuff right in front of me might help. I figured little harm could come from following his procedure, which more or less comes down to hot and cold hydrotherapy, although I'm sure his followers would call me out for that gross oversimplification.

I set up a hydrotherapy tank in my home, using my own water treatment method, which involves high ozone treatment coupled with medium pressure UV, which produces hydroxyl radicals in the process now widely known as "advanced oxidation process." Then, I started soaking every morning.

To be sure, I'm no doctor and I can't explain in any concrete terms why the soaking worked, but work it did. Within a very short time, all of my symptoms disappeared. In fact, in a matter of days I felt better than I ever had before in my entire life.

Why it Worked

Maybe it was purely psychological, or perhaps there's something to breathing water vapor, especially pristinely clean water vapor, or perhaps it's the effects of temperature. I honestly do not know, but I am certain that when I started soaking (a ritual I named my "Daily U"), I went from miserably ill to complete revitalization. Whether or not it's all in my head, it doesn't really matter. Fact is, Kneipp's water cure worked for me.

Nowadays, I still practice my Daily U and have always found it entirely enjoyable. I do it first thing in the morning, which is always a great start to the day. Because of the way I treat the water, it's always clean and crystal clear. I never have to worry about water quality, which at the very least removes a potential obstacle to enjoying the benefits. When I go from hot to cold and back again, I get a tingling feeling that runs from my head to my toes. There's no form of artificial stimulant that comes anywhere close to the wonderful natural high I experience every morning.

So, when I'm asked what motivates me, why I love the world of water so much, the answer is simple: I believe it probably saved my life or at the very least unquestionably improved my daily experience. I'd wager that most anyone who's had a similarly profound experience would feel much the same way.

Meet the Water Quality Manager

There is a solution

So, here's the big reveal, the main point of this book. For several years, and directly as a result of working service and construction, I've promoted the idea of establishing a new type of aquatic professional – the water quality manager (WQM).

Because water quality is the key factor for any type of aquatic property, commercial or residential, I believe it makes sense that our industry develop a class of professional who goes beyond the traditional role of a service technician.

I see a profile that includes equal parts consultant, troubleshooter and chemist; someone who understands sanitation, filtration, mineral balance, hydraulics and how all those things fit together. Such a professional amalgam would help facility owners and managers maintain their brand, ensure bather safety and comfort, and ultimately keep the doors open and their customers happy.

In other words, by ensuring topnotch water quality, the

WQM works to forge the level of quality experience people should expect when immersing their bodies in professionally maintained water. The WQM would leave nothing to chance by establishing systems that can withstand the rigors of high use. In doing so, he or she would become the guarantor of an experience that keeps people coming back to enjoy sparkling water that is wholesome and safe.

There are some big ideas embedded in this grand hypothetical, but for me the journey that led to my point of view had the most humble of beginnings. I started on pool service 30 years ago working out of a Volkswagen bug with no front passenger seat and a pole sticking out the window, maroon and utterly ridiculous looking. Fittingly, I had no idea what I was doing.

From the start, it dawned on me that people were counting on me to take care of their water, that in a very tangible way their health and safety was my responsibility. Their ability to safely enjoy the aquatic experience was in my hands.

I learned that lesson the hard way when at one point, a kid came down with a severe ear infection in one of my pools, which had poor water quality with algae and red mold. That was a major revelation because I knew this was serious business, and if I didn't get myself up to speed on managing water quality, I could really end up hurting somebody.

That's really where my focus began and my frustration, as well. On one hand, service professionals are charged with protecting everyone who goes in the pools they maintain. I view that as an almost sacred responsibility. It's a very important job, to say the least; people's health is at stake. But on the other, the industry itself was like a barren wasteland when it came to available information. Every time I asked questions, no one had an answer. Or so it seemed for a long time. The approach was to simply try out different products and see what worked. So, that's what I did, and I always felt like there was an ingredient missing. In the meantime, the water quality I was delivering was hit and miss.

One of our early big accounts was taking care of violinist Itzhak Perlman's massive pool. He good-naturedly once told me that although he had paid for the bottom of his pool, he had never seen it. The water quality was terrible, and all I knew to do at the time was keep hitting it with chlorine. In fact, I probably added 100 pounds of HTH to the water hoping it would eventually clear up, which it did, more or less, but I knew in my heart that couldn't be the best approach. There had to be a better way!

It took years to develop my knowledge to a point where I became confident treating and managing water quality. Through trial and error and a handful of reliable sources I did eventually find, I was able to create a systematic approach that works every time. Although I now consider myself an expert, there's still an abiding anxiety that comes as part of the profession. The bottom line is that people who own pools, be they public or private, are trusting someone else to know what they're doing. The problem is they have no way of knowing what the professional does and doesn't know.

In a very real way, the entire industry hinges on the credibility of those in charge of managing the water. It's so important that I believe we're long past due for a class of credentialed professional whose job it is to remove any doubt about the water's condition.

Imagine a World

I've always believed that to make something real, such as
the advent of the water quality professional (WQP), you first have
to visualize it. It's true in most, if not all, aspects of life. Creating a
different reality requires first seeing it in your mind's eye. Only then
can you begin taking the steps needed to make it real and affect
positive change. Right now, in terms of water quality management,
we've only visualized the very tip of the iceberg.

That's why when it comes to the state of recreational water
I'm an unashamed idealist. I've devoted my career to providing
people with water that is not only safe but also aesthetically pleasing.
Yes, it requires technical know-how, but ahead of the science and
technology, it's crucial to believe in the vision.

While the act of imaging based on idealism may seem a
romantic or even silly exercise to some cynics, truth be told, we
already live in a world overflowing with examples of visions becoming

truth. I think of Steve Jobs and how he said imagine a world where you have a music library in your pocket, or you can connect to the Internet through your phone, or even a world where everyone has a computer. He imagined those things and many more, which in turn drove the diligence that was required to develop today's digital technology and stoked the demand that made those products so historically successful.

My belief in artisan water stems from the fact that I've seen imagination become reality and I've seen how it impacts people. It's a beautiful vision and one that is, I believe, entirely attainable. The only thing holding us back, ultimately, is a reluctance to accept the notion that change is possible. So as we embark on this journey toward aquatic excellence, let's take a moment to think about what we're trying to achieve.

Imagine a world where pool water doesn't smell, where being inside an indoor aquatic facility doesn't mean enduring the familiar and sometimes overwhelming chloramine odor. Imagine a world where kids don't need inhalers just to get through a workout, or suffer breathing problems later on.

Imagine a world where pool water is just as reliable as drinking water, where you can be sure that when you or your kids go swimming in a public facility, you know there are standards being met for overall water quality. It's a world where water balance, sanitation, and the destruction of disinfection by-products are a given, where the water never gets so bad that facilities have to be shut down while it's set right.

Imagine a world where facility owners and managers invest

in their brand by way of ensuring water that protects their customers' health and keeps them wanting to come back for more, where they don't have to fear a visit from the local health inspector.

Imagine a world where those same managers and owners understand that it's in their own best interest and the interest of their customers and constituents to invest in quality water treatment.

Imagine a world where no one ever gets sick from using a swimming pool. Where the terms "water-related illness" and "*Cryptosporidium*" are obsolete. Think about what would happen to the restaurant industry if every time you went out to eat, you had to worry there was a possibility that dining out might make you sick. That's unthinkable in the restaurant industry, yet, in the world of aquatics, risk of illness is an accepted part of the equation.

Imagine a world where people of all ages can more fully benefit from living an aquatic lifestyle. Think about the benefits to health and fitness, both physical and mental, and how swimming and exercising in water can positively impact the lives of our children, as well as ourselves. When you don't have to worry about the wholesomeness of the water itself, you're inevitably far freer to make swimming a part of your routine.

Imagine a world where the health and safety of everyone using pools and spas is safeguarded by a class of professionals, specifically water quality professionals, who have studied the arts and sciences of water chemistry, filtration, hydraulics, and system control.

Imagine a world where the increased demand for aquatic facilities results in new pools being built rather than old ones being abandoned.

Imagine a world where all of these concepts are well established, where excellence in water quality management is the norm and not exceptional.

Of course, as it stands now, we're a long way from that world. The pool, spa, and aquatics industry does have professionals who think this way, but it's far from everyone in the business. Likewise, people who own and operate aquatic facilities are often not versed enough in water quality management to appreciate that the resources they devote to maintaining artisan water will pay back multi-fold. Perhaps the first step in changing the world of aquatics is simply imagining how fortifying it would be if we thought differently about the future. Dreams can become reality if we're serious about making a positive change. It's encouraging, too, that it all can start today with just a small dose of imagination.

Healthy Water in the Realm of the Senses

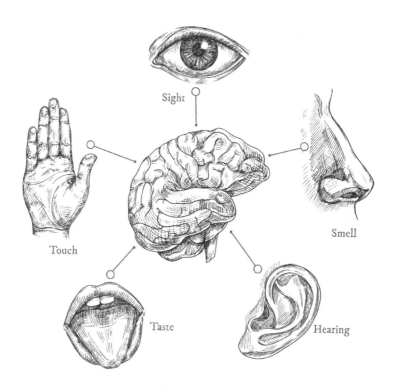

Sight

Touch

Smell

Taste

Hearing

As is true of most endeavors in which us humans diligently apply ourselves, the art and science of recreational water treatment become more complex and sophisticated as time goes along. Yet, for all of the sanitizing, filtration, balance and testing methods at our disposal these days, you don't really need to know anything about those technologies to know whether or not things are right.

Truth is, we have all the tools we need to determine whether or not there's some kind of problem. Our eyes, ears, nose, mouth, and skin constantly gather data, and they are infinitely more sophisticated than our man-made information-gathering implements.

As important, our five senses, to which I would personally add basic human intuition as the elusive sixth sense, will tell us when we're in a wholesome environment, but only if we first get in the habit of paying attention.

That may sound overly simplistic, but in truth I believe one of the obstacles to achieving artisanal water conditions is that it's in our nature to learn to ignore what our senses tell us. It happens in an infinite number of ways: pushing aside your back pain to get your work done, averting your eyes when you drive by a neighbor's house who never clears the piles of trash on the lawn, or learning to ignore unpleasant smells you routinely experience, like the chlorine stench at your community center pool.

As the cliché goes, the first step in fixing a problem is realizing you have one. In the realm of all things aquatic that means first paying attention to your senses. It works when things are awry and also to help confirm when the water is dialed in.

Sight

This one is easy. If the pool water is not clear, if it's cloudy, if there is visible dirt and debris floating in the water or on the pool floor, if there are dead bugs, or live ones in and around the water, if there's trash on the deck, all are indications of different types of problems. Same is true for visible corrosion, staining, scale, or rust on surfaces and components. If you see inhalers all over the pool deck because kids are having trouble breathing and for heaven's sake, if a pool light is flickering, these are powerful warning signs that something is wrong. Bottom line: don't ignore what you see.

Sound

This is a little tricky. Pool systems are, or at least should be, made to run silently, so when you hear louder than usual mechanical noises coming from the equipment, it's almost certainly time for a service call with a qualified technician. Some noise is normal so you need to become accustomed to the sounds of the system operating properly.

But there's another level; that is, hearing what people say about their experience. And that's where the lost art of listening comes into play. I'm always impressed with the way children pick up on things that us grown-ups sometimes miss. When it comes to conditions in an aquatic facility, indoors or outside, it pays to listen to what young swimmers tell you about the experience. Phrases like "It stinks," "My eyes burn," or "My skin itches," are powerful indicators that should trigger the savvy pool operator or water quality professional to suspect elevated levels of disinfection by-products, and sanitizer demand that is outrunning the treatment method. Kids are like those canaries in coalmines, especially in pools, because they are very sensory oriented, have less cluttered minds, and walk around with less developed social filters, that is, they say what they experience.

Suffice it to say when I hear kids complain, it's time to break out the test kit.

Smell

Right there with sight, this is the easiest to grasp, even though it's the sense that most of us probably use the least. When you or others get a whiff of the familiar chloramine smell, the water needs help. It could be that the smelly vessel is being refilled with source water that's treated with monochloramine, or the system simply isn't keeping up with demand, or a combination of both.

The facility might need a completely revamped treatment system, perhaps turning away from chlorine-only treatment to incorporate ozone and/or UV technology. Or there could be other measures, like paying more attention to kids showering prior to entering the water, or encouraging bathroom breaks. Whatever the type of remediation, staring down that path often first goes through the nose.

Taste

Pool water should have no taste, just like drinking water. Another basic indicator, if the water tastes bad, it's time to look for the issue. It's not surprising that bad smelling and bad tasting water often go hand in hand.

Touch

Pool surfaces and components are created to be smooth and easy on the touch. If you find rough patches on the surface or abrasive edges on components like rails or ladders, something's not right. Certainly, touch comes into play after you get out of the water. Dry, rough, or itchy skin, or red and burning eyes, should never be part of the aquatic experience. If someone feels any level of electrical shock, it's time to close the pool and carefully inspect the electrical service, bonding, and grounding connections.

Touch also works on an entirely different level; one that I personally suspect might be at least part or maybe even entirely psychological. In my experience, with the "gourmet" way I treat pools, many clients and pool users have reported that they love the way the water feels, that there's a perceptible quality to the texture that enhances their enjoyment.

Although I love hearing those remarks because it means they're having a positive experience, I don't honestly know if different treatment methods create different types of "feels" to the water.

I do suspect that when water is clean, properly sanitized, and balanced, when it's odorless and tasteless, when it's a comfortable temperature and especially when it looks beautiful, there are no distractions to the enjoyment. I liken it to the way a freshly cleaned car seems to run better. We know rationally that the car doesn't run differently because it's been cleaned, but when it's looking spiffy and smelling fresh we often get the feeling the ride is a little smoother as well.

Is that naiveté or simply the nature of sensory experience? Our mind processes the information we receive through our senses and forms an impression of the experience we're currently experiencing. Does water that's treated perfectly actually feel different? Frankly, I'm not sure it really matters. What does matter is that the people who turn to the water for health and recreation walk away feeling refreshed, relaxed and rejuvenated.

For those of us who spend our working lives making sure that people who turn to water for health and recreation walk away feeling good, it only makes sense to start in the realm of the senses.

Educating Ourselves on Water Quality

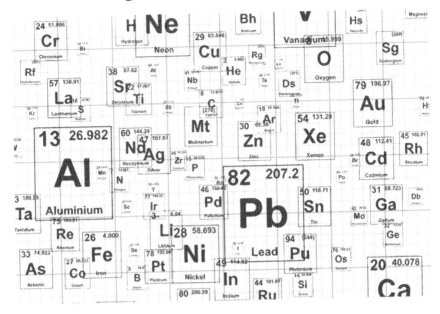

For as long as I've worked in the aquatics industry, there's always been a tremendous amount of talk, and complaining, about "education." The basic patter is that our industry lacks formal educational opportunities, and if we want to be successful, both individually and as an industry, we have to up our game.

While I generally agree with that having experienced my own struggles finding reliable information, especially about pool chemistry, I also believe the key to elevating our knowledge begins at home, so to speak, with each of us individually and within our own companies. Ultimately, education is a self-determined process. Those who seek it will find it, those who don't, never will. The plain fact is, you can sit in a class taught by the world's greatest instructor, but if you don't pay attention, you might as well be playing solitaire. By contrast, someone with seemingly little opportunity but who is determined to learn will almost always find a way.

The irony is, however, that while education does start with a personal decision to learn, it is also very much a process of collaboration, and that's especially true inside a company culture.

I've always taken great pride in the fact that our company has an intense focus on learning and that our staff is populated by people who have been trained and educated in great detail about the nuances of building and servicing beautiful bodies of water. They are the ones who, through their talent and skill sets, ultimately create the client experience; and that's a fact that we actively promote as a benefit of doing business with our company.

Elevating Everyone

What I find fascinating and inspiring about the educational process is how it creates balance in our organization. In our staff of 12 full-time, year-round employees, each person brings different strengths to the formula. We have people who are great at solving technical problems, those who are better at customer relations, some are better at developing reliable procedures, some are wildly creative while others are more cautious. When you combine those differing attributes with established bodies of knowledge, that is, education, then you start to unlock both the potential of the individual and the alchemy of organizational success.

As the head honcho of our company, I've embraced the concept that education starts with me personally. After all, you can't teach what you don't know and by way of my own efforts to educate myself, I am then able to cull resources and develop specific protocols that can be taught and reinforced in the workplace. In other words, because I've empowered myself with knowledge, I am now able to do the same for others.

I know from experience working with other organizations and getting to know people in all walks of life that collaboration and empowerment through education are not as common as they should be. There are companies that limit what they teach employees, sometimes out of fear of training future competition, or perhaps for not wanting to give up the power that comes with being the only source of knowledge.

What I see in those cultures is more centralized authority and decision-making, all of which breeds reluctance to assume responsibility, intellectual stagnation and, sometimes, even paranoia. Autocratic business leaders, especially those who see potential limits or even threats in educating others, miss opportunities to create efficiencies, a positive work environment, positive customer relations, and ultimately effective problem solving.

For my part, I'm thrilled that my most experienced people, both on the service and building sides, know as much as I do. Because we've invested in their acumen, they can take ownership of issues in the field, develop solutions to problems, and deal directly with our clients.

Nowadays, that store of information is pretty darn impressive. We have specific procedures and info on a galaxy of topics such as calculating hydraulics, water balance, doing plaster start-ups, how to close a pool for winter and open one in spring, and dozens of other specifics that ultimately enable us to make all the pieces of a system work together. And even though we have literally volumes of information in our company library, we also recognize that we don't know everything and that education is always an ongoing process.

Ease of Confidence

In effect, a well-trained staff becomes an extension of your hand and one that ultimately thinks for him or herself. There's a kind of chain reaction that starts with education. Information leads to competence, competence leads to success, success leads to confidence, and confidence leads to a sense of purpose and comfort. Put another way, education is the nutrient that drives the entire food chain of achievement.

Yes, education starts with the individual, but it also encompasses the power to touch everyone around us, from our best employees and co-workers to the customers themselves. Education is truly the grandest of collaborations!

Why Prevention Instead of Reaction?

One of the key distinctions of professional water quality management, perhaps the most critical difference with the industry's status quo, is that it is – as I envision it, at least – proactive instead of reactive. When applied correctly, the arts and sciences of water quality management are ultimately all about avoiding problems before they happen, not after the fact.

Sounds simple enough, that is until we consider that the pool and spa service profession has traditionally been oriented toward responding to problems rather than taking preventive action to head them off in the first place. For example, service technicians as well as certified pool operators will test water to be sure it is in a state of mineral balance. Often, it's only when the pH drops or rises out of range, or the total alkalinity or calcium hardness are too low or too high do they take corrective measures.

I contend that if you get to the point where the water is

out of balance, you've already compromised the system in terms of corrosion, scale, or sanitizer inefficiency. We know for a settled fact that when water is imbalanced, a host of potential problems can and will ensue. Therefore, it seems logical that we should be employing technology that constantly monitors key mineral constituents and either automatically makes adjustments, and/or pings the pool operator that the water balance is shifting, before it actually becomes a problem.

This same principle of prevention versus reaction becomes even more critical when it comes to sanitization and oxidation. The simplest example, when sanitizer levels drop due to high bather loads and other forms of organic loading, adding chlorine or other sanitizers to catch back up to the demand is too late. The system should be resilient enough to never let sanitizer and oxidizer levels dip below a pre-determined level. That's how it works in public water utilities and industrial applications, and so too it should be the way our industry operates, as well. Unfortunately, for the most part, it's simply not the case.

Staying Ahead

The same is especially true of disinfection by-products, such as chloramines that form as a result of chlorine oxidizing organic compounds. If you come to the point that chloramines are generating the familiar and distasteful "chlorine smell" or causing burning eyes, or resulting in cloudy water, then the water quality is already compromised. By using technologies such as ozone, UV, and even AOP generation, as well as small concentrations of chlorine, we are able to prevent the accumulation of disinfection by-products so that the water never needs to be shocked or super-chlorinated.

When we caste our work in a preventive mold, we avoid insults to the consumer experience, and we avoid the costs of downtime and bruised reputations. We prevent fear and reluctance to go in the water and we ultimately enhance the consumer experience, which is the main point of the aquatics industry in the first place.

All of this means thinking differently about how we approach the work and tools we use in water quality management. It also means taking a more active role in communicating the value of water quality to those who benefit from investing in the technology that enables preventive maintenance.

This same concept extends to repairs, where anticipating replacement and equipment upgrades is part of the established service regimen. It also goes for filter cleaning, control system testing and calibration, and tile and surface cleaning and repair.

In a very real sense, we can assume that if water touches it, we can reasonably anticipate the need to mitigate problems before they inevitably occur. If we wait to address issues when they become evident, in most cases, we've waited too long.

Bottom line: prevention is professional, reaction is often something else.

Extending a Hand

Water treatment and the resulting water quality it does – or does not – provide are issues at the very heart of all aquatic facilities. The water is the essence, the lifeblood of places where people take the plunge. But there's far more to it than simply managing the rigors of chemistry, hydraulics, filtration, and control.

Water quality professionals also need to be sensitive to the human element. In this context, I'm not so much talking about the experience of those using the water, per se (crucial though it may be), but rather the nature of working with the people who manage and maintain a given property. Quite simply, I've come to understand and appreciate that success in treating water also means building and managing relationships.

In this industry and elsewhere, I've seen how some companies take the opposite approach and use fear with impunity to sell whatever it is they do – everything from fighting bad breath to why you need your roof repaired. It's all about fear, or to borrow a popular term these days, avoiding "pain points."

I've certainly seen that approach in various areas of the pool, spa, and aquatics industries, especially where health and safety are concerned.

Rather than stress the risks of waterborne diseases and disinfection by-products, I believe it's far more effective to empower the dialogue with the whys and hows involved in making positive change.

I see water quality problems as opportunities to improve the aquatic experience, and not as sources of fear. Because water is so integral to every type of aquatic facility, altering the treatment methods and site conditions can be an extremely intrusive process. There is the cost of corrective measures, the logistics of revamping systems, the permitting and approval processes and – always – overcoming reservations. It's human nature to resist change, and there are almost always people involved who are vested in maintaining the status quo. To some, accepting change is equal to admitting failure and that can be a very hard reservation to overcome.

How the water quality professional navigates the tricky human currents can often have as much bearing on the success of a project as does the technology itself. That's why I always approach all staff at aquatic facilities with a feeling of respect for their work and positions in a given organization. Even if the water quality itself is badly inferior, I'm only ever there to help, not to chastise, criticize, or condemn.

The Opportunity of Healthy Water

In many situations, I meet facility managers, property superintendents, or maintenance personnel who've been working at their facilities for 20 or more years. These are the people who know where the proverbial skeletons are hidden, the nuances and idiosyncrasies of the property and its history. They hold the church keys and as such can provide you the access you'll need, or they can keep you on the outside looking in.

For that reason and many others, I always represent my potential role in improving water quality as one of collaboration and offering solutions. I'm an extension of their hand, only there to assist with my own set of skills and specialized knowledge. My work exists only to protect a company's brand and their customers' health, to help everyone involved come out ahead.

Working with aquatic facilities is almost always a long-term proposition. Because improving water quality can mean spending a lot of time and money as well as accepting change, simply securing the contract can take a long, long time. As professionals marketing our services, we must be patient.

There will always be challenges in forging the human connection, that's a given, but it all starts by simply extending your hand.

Active Listening

Building those relationships also means opening your ears and mastering the lost art of listening.

Back in 2017, I had the pleasure of attending the 14th-Annual World Aquatic Health Conference in Denver, Colorado. It was the second time I've made it to the event, which is produced by the National Swimming Pool Foundation. Like the first time around, I found the experience incredibly stimulating and inspiring.

As the name suggests, the WAHC is about all things aquatic and health related. It's a wonderful forum for people like me who are devoted to designing, building, managing, and maintaining quality aquatic facilities. Again at the '17 installment, I spent quality time in the company of professionals with common goals of promoting aquatics and elevating the industry through science and shared information.

The keynote speaker was Ryan Avery, the youngest-ever

Toastmasters champion, a brilliant young man with a strong message about the power of effective communication. His presentation focused on how we convey to others what it is we have to offer, both collectively and individually. It was one of those discussions that could apply to a wide range of industries but happens to be particularly well suited for the world of aquatics.

The Need to Communicate Effectively

Avery captured my full attention, and I immediately started thinking about how important effective communication and constructive idea exchange is to everything we do, professionally and personally. It's how we reflect our determination, develop teamwork, and ultimately build a community. Taken together, all of those qualities drive confidence.

It also struck me that a huge part of communicating effectively is not only what we say and how we choose to say it but also as important is how effectively we listen. I often find myself thinking that we become so focused on getting our point across that we almost reflexively forget to listen. In the world of aquatics, and especially in the work of the WQM, the ability and willingness to first open our ears should be considered an essential part of the job.

Unfortunately, I believe that as an industry we've largely ignored the most important voices in the entire equation: those of the end users.

It's a common shortfall throughout society but particularly so in the world of aquatics. Collectively, we've done a lousy job of listening to what our customers are telling us. In a sense, not listening to our consumers is like trying to manage water chemistry without testing it first. It's fundamentally impossible to identify a problem and a course of remediation without some type of feedback loop. That's a shortcoming that applies to facility owners and managers as well as aquatic professionals of all stripes from pool operators, to engineers, to lifeguards. Everyone at all levels of the industry would do well to work on actively listening to our consumers.

Part of why I feel so strongly about this is because the problem first came into focus for me as a consumer, not as a professional. When my kids started experiencing significant respiratory problems as a result of swimming at a local public pool facility, no one from the facility or anyone else in the industry would listen. It was maddening, and from then on I've known that our industry needs to up its game on a variety of fronts – from facility management, to water treatment, to air quality, to basic cleanliness.

Listen to Customer Feedback

We all know that every facility is different with its own set of challenges across a range of potential issues. The best way to know where to improve is to listen to those who are using what we have to offer. Otherwise, it's all just guesswork. Without active listening, we are throwing the proverbial darts blindfolded. As I've mentioned before, I come from the restaurant business. I can't imagine how unreasonable and impossible success would have been had we not listened to the people paying their hard-earned dollars to eat our food.

Yet, we all know it's human nature to set aside the critique of others because it's usually easier, at least in the moment, to dismiss a complaint rather than to stop what you're doing and take some kind of corrective action. Consider what most likely happens to a comment that a parent shares with a lifeguard. We know that casual feedback is often lost the moment it's spoken, or at best distorted when it gets passed along.

The wonderful flipside of this "listening deficit" are the opportunities that do exist when we deliberately open our ears and choose to pay attention to customer feedback. Not only can we more closely identify pertinent problems and thus correct them with greater speed and efficiency, we also empower the consumer and build on that magic word: confidence.

We have everything to gain. By engaging our audience, we become more confident in our ability to provide quality aquatic experiences and, in turn, we inspire confidence in those we seek to serve.

The Art of Service

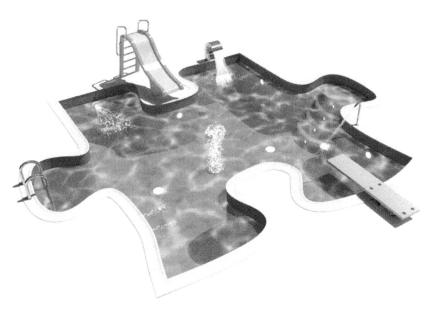

Pool and spa service may not be the most glamorous job, but for those of us who've made it our profession, it can be nothing short of an art form. Having experienced the benefits of artisan water, and witnessed the perils of poorly maintained water, I view service and water quality management as a truly awesome responsibility.

The work involves a variety of interrelated tasks and goals that require consistent and careful attention. There's chemistry, hydraulics, mechanics, problem solving, customer relations, and even being a good driver – all wrapped into one job that can challenge even the most experienced practitioners.

Service work is where all the intertwined facets of pool design, engineering, and technology come together. When all systems and routines are running smoothly, pools and spas stay clean, healthy, and inviting. When service spins out of the grooves, pools turn green, cloudy, smell bad, and can become unsafe. There's tremendous responsibility that comes with the job in that our clients depend on us to be sure their pools and spas are always ready to use, biologically and chemically safe, and always inviting.

Suffice to say it's a much bigger set of challenges than most people tend to think.

As is true of pools themselves, all service businesses are a little bit different. Our company services about 300 mostly residential pools, in addition to our work building custom pools and spas. Here on Long Island it's seasonal work, meaning we close up pools in the fall and re-open them in spring, and we shut down operations during the coldest months. Most of the properties we work on are vacation homes, meaning there's a huge ebb and flow over the weekends.

All of our accounts are within a five-mile radius of our shop, a luxury of working in a densely populated and relatively affluent area. From an operations standpoint, we're able to do more in less time simply because our technicians are not spending much time between stops.

I've been working in service for more than 30 years and am the first to admit that it took me a long time to completely figure out how all the puzzle pieces fit together and the best way to structure our service routines. In many ways, service is the art of organizing the obvious while at the same time solving the unknown. It's a great way to learn the nuances of applied chemistry and get a great suntan all at the same time.

It's the kind of customer-facing work where to be successful you have to approach each and every account, and every client, as though they're your only one. That's why we treat every client the way we would want to be treated ourselves, as if it were our kids swimming in the waters for which we care. Maintaining that value system requires a constant state of readiness and dedication to quality. No problem is too small or too big for us to handle and we always respond as quickly as possible.

As I mentioned previously, we take the same approach to service as my family did in the restaurant business. We are providing a quality experience that meets customer expectations every time. We know we are in the pleasure business and in essence it's our job to ensure nothing on the waterfront disrupts the clients' quest for "the good life."

One Thing Leads to Another

The overarching principle in quality service is to understand how each facet of the work influences every other part of the job. Using our work as an example, it's interesting how the end of every season sets the stage for the next. The way we treat the water and close down the system in the fall will have everything to do with what we have to contend with when we come back and open our pools in the spring.

Each year, prior to opening our pools, we work with our clients to make necessary repairs and upgrades to their systems. We want all the filters clean and all pumps, motors, heaters, and chemical feeders in perfect operating condition. That way, when we pull all those winterizing covers off the water, the systems are fully operational.

Opening pools is one of the more challenging aspects of pool service. Because of the careful way we chemically treat the water at closing, about 80 percent of our pools are crystal clear when we open them. Still, there are always some that have turned cloudy or green. The exact processes we use to correct those water quality problems are surprisingly complicated. We're always refining how we correct water balance, shock the water if necessary, cycle the filter, vacuum and brush, raise sanitizer levels, and the sequences in which we do all of those things.

Some pools temporarily require daily care to bring them back to useable conditions; while others are basically ready to go once we raise the water level and re-adjust the chemistry.

Once all our pools are open, we fall into a steady rhythm over the remaining months of spring, through the summer and into the fall. Admittedly our business is different than many others because so many of our clients are here only over the weekends. That means when they arrive on Thursday and Friday, their pools and spa have to be ready to rock.

When they leave, we get back to work on Monday by visiting every one of our accounts to assess the water quality and make chemical adjustments with micro-shock treatments if there's been heavy use and also to adjust water balance. Then, the rest of the week we spend with the cleaning regimens and making any repairs as needed.

It's a constant cycle that is based on both steady routines and improvisation as we contend with unexpected issues and client requests.

Building for Service

Our decades of experience on the service side of the business have been intrinsically valuable in our design and construction work. In fact, I moved into construction precisely because I could see how the way a pool is set up from the start influences how easy or difficult it is to service.

Simple things, like arranging skimmers and returns so there are no dead spots, or organizing the equipment pad so that everything is accessible, or properly sizing the plumbing and components so that everything runs quietly and efficiently, all of those basic measures and many others are crucial throughout the life of the system.

It's interesting to think that every pool and every spa is essentially a miniature water treatment system. On one hand pool and spa systems are not entirely dissimilar from the systems that treat our public water supplies, or on a much smaller scale, they also have a lot in common with home aquariums. Regardless of scale, the principles of filtration, chemical treatment, and proper maintenance remain relatively the same.

From a builder perspective, it's helpful to know that the pool and its treatment system will be serviced in a way that will increase the service life of the components, preserve the pool's appearance and above all, provide the experience the homeowners are paying for in the first place. That's why I always say I'd prefer to service pools I build and build the pools we'll service.

When a well-built pool is serviced correctly, only then are we truly able to deliver a consistency of product that meets client expectations. Experience has taught that when you get it all right, when you make all the pieces fit together like a beautifully written symphony, or a delicious recipe, service may not be the sexiest occupation, but it is very, very satisfying because ultimately we're making people happy!

Testing the Waters

It's the key that unlocks the door: in one way or another water quality management always circles back to chemistry. Managing water quality is, very much, an exercise in manipulating chemical values so that water remains sanitized, balanced, and appealing.

The only way to do that — to ply the trade of the WQP — is to be proficient in water testing. Whether it's through traditional reagent-based tests in vials, or test strips or electronic testing technology, testing is our eyes into the chemistry of the water we're managing. You simply cannot separate testing from water chemistry or vice versa. In a practical sense, one does not really exist without the other.

Early Learning

When I started in the business three decades ago, I had very little idea of what I was doing, and although I tried to find reliable information sources, they were few and far between. That was until I started reading the *Taylor Technologies Guidebook*, a wonderful resource published by one of the leading manufacturers of testing technology. That single publication not only explained how to test water but also gave me the foundation for the entirety of pool and spa water chemical treatment.

I quickly learned that through simple tests for pH, total alkalinity, calcium hardness, TDS, and cyanuric acid as well as testing for combined and free available chlorine, I was able to watch the causes and effects of the chemicals I was adding. All of a sudden, I could see what a dynamic beast water chemistry can be, how it changes and reacts and how the measurable differences in chemical constituents impact each other. Through water testing, we can see how animated pools and other bodies of water become.

Even the most basic aspects of water treatment became eye opening. If I added calcium hypochlorite, I could test and see that my calcium levels would increase. In terms of water balance, I could see how by adding acid, total alkalinity and pH would go down. Then I could see how by adding bicarbonate the pH would go back up. Everything we do to the water has a cause-and-effect relationship. It's impossible to ascertain any of that without routine testing that is done correctly and reliably.

At the Source

Later on, I discovered how important it is to test source water at the tap. To this day, I'm amazed how some people try to manage water chemistry without first understanding how the water we use to fill vessels creates a baseline that influences the chemistry going forward. I learned, for example, that water in one area can be completely different from another area just a few miles away.

Through my basic testing regimens, I learned that water in one place might change over time, meaning it's important to never make assumptions that things will always stay the same. And I learned how the balance of tap water, as well as how it's sanitized, can directly impact what you need to do once it's added to the pool.

If that was all there is to it, water testing would be arguably one of, if not the most important, aspects of water quality management, but these days, what we can do with test goes so much further. With today's automatic testing technology, we can set up systems that will give us a heads up of problems coming our way, and we can use the information from that technology to develop treatment systems that are resilient to high bather use.

Using Ozone and UV

In my own work, I've spent years perfecting systems that utilize ozone and UV systems along with very low levels of chlorine residuals. The testing/monitoring systems that accompany that technology are at the heart of everything I've done along these lines.

Quite a lot has been made these days of the advanced oxidation process (AOP). It's fairly complex chemistry, but in a nutshell, AOP refers to a process where ozone and UV light are combined to create hydroxyl radicals, which are highly oxidative oxygen species that exist in solution for only a tiny fraction of a second. Even though hydroxyl radicals exist for less than a blink of an eye, they are among the most effective oxidizers known to science. Also, because they are so short-lived, it is impossible to directly test for their existence. There is no AOP test kit and probably never will be.

Over the years I've learned that you can, however, essentially confirm the existence of hydroxyl radicals by testing the oxidation reduction potential (ORP) before and after the UV system. When ozone is generated, it dramatically increases ORP. When it flows through the UV system, ozone is destroyed and transformed into hydroxyl radicals, which do not register as ORP because of their almost instantaneous reaction time. Therefore, when we see the ORP drop after ozonated water flows through a UV system, we can reliably deduce that the combination of ozone and UV is, in fact, creating hydroxyl radicals.

Employing UVT and UVA

Making effective use of UV systems also means embracing a couple types of testing that are, for the most part, unfamiliar to many people in the pool and spa industry. They are two interrelated values known as ultraviolet transmittance (UVT) and ultraviolet absorbance (UVA).

UVT is the measure of how much light passes through a water sample relative to how much light would pass through a "pure" water sample, expressed in a percentage. Pure water will have a UVT value of 100 percent, while totally opaque water has a value of 0 percent. The higher the value, the more light is passing through the water, meaning there are lesser concentrations of organics and other compounds that absorb light, or disrupt the transmittance.

UVA essentially measures the same thing, but rather than working via transmittance it measures the relative amount of light absorbed. Both measurements are used to calculate and control the output of a UV system, which in the case of a water treatment system is on the 254nm wavelength.

Putting it All Together

When you combine UVT, UVA, and ORP testing, you can set up a system that makes the most out of UV and ozone treatment methods. That all might sound like a far cry from standard reagent testing for pH, total alkalinity, calcium hardness, and sanitizer demand, but the idea is basically the same. You use testing technology and results to manage the treatment so the system never falls behind the demand on sanitizers and oxidizers relative to bather load and other sources of contaminants.

And, in these systems, I'll use a familiar ppm testing for chlorine for bather-to-bather contacts, as well as pH to maintain balanced conditions.

The precise design of these systems and where the different tests are taken in the plumbing depends largely on the situation, and I'll stop short of going into those explanations, which could take up a discussion several times this length.

Suffice to say that how we use water testing has come a long way, but at its core, there is nothing more essential to the successful treatment of water.

From the French

There's a saying in French cooking that I've always loved: *mise en place.*

Translated it means, "everything in its place," or as I was taught in culinary school, "the state of readiness." In practice, *mise en place* simply means being prepared to cook; having the kitchen set with all cookware, accouterments, and ingredients ready to rock-n-roll.

I contend there's a direct parallel in creating and maintaining top-shelf bodies of water, a *mise en place aquatique.* That might sound fancy, as many French phrases do, but it's really just common sense. When all the pieces in an aquatic system complement and support each other – hydraulics, chemical treatment, control technology, filtration, heating and, often, automatic pool covers – the water stays clean and safe, is far more easily maintained, and is usually so at reduced costs.

Having been indoctrinated by my culinary instructors to the concept of readiness, I've come to approach aquatic design, construction, and maintenance the same way. I believe the best way to ensure a pool system is synergistic is to design and build it yourself so that you know it's in a state of readiness.

As a result, the pools we design and construct are not only beautiful but also remarkably easy to maintain, and it's all because we've made sure everything is in its place.

The "Idea House Water Quality Challenge"

In all, I worked for just shy of 20 years in service before moving into design and construction. We had become proficient in repairs, minor to major, but it wasn't until 2007 I designed and built our first original project. It all started when *Hamptons Cottage and Gardens Magazine* contacted us with an offer to participate in an "Idea House" project, which the publication was sponsoring.

The concept was to create a home that maximized energy efficiency, embodied environmental stewardship, and reflected state-of-the-art design and construction.

For our part, the magazine challenged us to create a pool with beautiful water quality that didn't use *any* chlorine. As unconventional as that idea has traditionally been, my experience in service had led me to believe that with the right system in place, eliminating chlorine altogether was, indeed, possible.

I learned a lot on that project, to say the least. Among the most important revelations was my belief in the power of the ozone / UV combination, which we'll discuss in greater detail. I also developed the approach of running the sanitizing and oxidizing systems on separate sets of returns on opposite sides of the pool, with two sets of three skimmers maximizing cleaning and creating circulation through the vessel.

The Idea House was open with daily tours throughout the summer of 2008. The pool was a terrific success and our work designing and building bodies of water had begun. It was an exciting time to say the least.

Design, Build, Maintain

In the years since, we've continued to learn how the decisions builders make have an almost incalculable combined impact on the way a pool operates and the level of maintenance it requires.

In one of the more obvious examples, the builder chooses the chemical treatment system. For numerous reasons, that decision alone stands as one of the most pivotal of all. It influences everything else that happens in the water. In our practice, we turn to differing versions of ozone / UV and small amounts of chlorine on the vast majority of projects.

Although a number of factors influence the design of each system – source water, anticipated bather load, indoor versus outdoor, dirt and debris, even the presence of birds – the objective of readiness always remains the same. The conditions surrounding and impacting each body of water similarly dictate the type of filtration, pump selection, turnover rate, the number and placement of skimmers, the interior finish, hardscape materials, the plumbing layout, heating, and the control system.

There are countless examples of how everything works together; consider the synergies of using an automatic pool cover, as one. A cover prevents dirt and debris from entering the pool and retains heat by reducing evaporation. An automatic safety cover also prevents accidents. It saves money, reduces chemical demand, and extends the swim season by making heating more cost effective. That's quite a list stemming from one lone decision of whether or not to cover the pool.

The same kind of benefit can be found in a properly designed plumbing layout. If cherry trees surround a pool, common in much of the Northeast, we'll increase the number of skimmers. Service techs all know how valuable adequate skimming action is, especially when something like cherry blossoms fall into the water in large quantities. In all pools, we work to create complete circulation distribution, which dramatically increases the effectiveness of most any type of chemical treatment. Likewise, even distribution increases heating efficiency. It all works together.

Control systems offer a different type of synergistic benefits. Not only does chemical control work wonders to maintain ongoing water quality, which dramatically reduces maintenance and extends the life of pool equipment and surfaces, today's systems also communicate. Being able to see what's going on with a pool operation on a smartphone or other device saves time and travel distance. When problems arise, it's usually as simple as the power had been turned off, but we know how frustrating it is to travel miles to flip a switch. And when there's a serious issue, we can respond before the water quality degrades.

In these ways, design decisions directly influence the experience and expense of maintaining pools and spas of all types. When you stop and think about it, there's a beautiful power found in embracing *mise en place*!

A Top-Shelf Seminar

Periodic Table of the Elements

It's no secret that at times I've been critical of the state of education in the aquatics/pool/spa industry, as I have in previous chapters here. It's not my nature to complain; yet throughout my long tenure in the industry, I've consistently found it difficult to find adequate informational resources – a shortcoming that has become a common refrain among many in our profession.

That's why when I do find a great source of information, it's refreshing to point it out and give credit where due. Case in point, I had the pleasure of attending a tremendous advanced water chemistry seminar presented by chemist Ellen Meyer of chemistry manufacturing giant, Lonza. The session was part of an otherwise impressive educational docket at that year's Atlantic City Pool & Spa Show.

Meyer is a terrific instructor and easily one of the most knowledgeable experts I've ever encountered in the pool and spa chemistry. What set her presentation apart from others I've attended was the way that she connected all the dots and did so based on hard data, years of scientific inquiry, and experience in the field. To my mind, whenever you're delving into water chemistry, it's always about the science.

Everything has an action and reaction; everything holds hands in one way or another. If you look at the science through the right perspective, you can find strengths and weaknesses in the patterns, which is the basis for advancement and ultimately an improved bather experience.

That's what Meyer did so artfully, she not only comprehensively covered the major elements of recreational water chemistry but also made sure her audience came away with an understanding of how all those pieces fit together. For anyone who's taken on the challenge of managing water in a high-use aquatic facility, it becomes immediately obvious that the factors you're manipulating do not function in isolation but are always interdependent. She did a spectacular job of illustrating those relationships.

In Deep

Among the many topical highlights, she discussed bather load (capacity) issues, water-related disease outbreaks, and how the CDC's Model Aquatic Health Code is designed to stymie waterborne diseases. She talked about bacteria, including *Pseudomonas*, *E. coli*, and *Legionella*, the *Norovirus*, and the many other organisms that make people sick. She covered how those come about and what we need to do to prevent outbreaks, including detailed information about contact times and different types of sanitizers such as UV, ozone, and the different types of chlorine. Part of the presentation was also dedicated to algae and prevention, as well as information about cyanuric acid.

For a three-and-a-half hour presentation, Meyer was about as comprehensive as possible. She did a great job of backing up her points with hard science while also speaking about the limitations of testing in labs versus real-world field experience. She implored us to work with chemical manufacturers so they can base product development and recommended applications with both lab science and what happens in bodies of water filled with people and influenced by the countless variables.

Ultimately, the information she presented fused science with the objectives of the Model Aquatic Health Code as well as the *Guidelines for Safe Recreational Water Environments*, volume 2, published by the World Health Organization in 2006. All in all, Meyer's seminar was a prime example of the level of information our industry desperately needs.

Controlling the Tipping Point

You don't have to be a high profile "thought leader" to know that water has both a light and a dark side. On one hand, we know all about the existential importance of water as a natural resource, we simply cannot live without it. And, we know that water provides a spectrum of recreational activities and aesthetic appeal that can't be found anywhere else. Aquatic activity is arguably both the healthiest and most enjoyable of all forms of leisure and recreation.

For all of that profound virtue, water can also be incredibly dangerous. For starters, humans are not designed for the life aquatic. We are land animals who have adapted to water, love the water, but are also exceedingly vulnerable when we step off of dry land. Also, excessive rainfall causes floods that can wreak incalculable property damage, injury, and death, just as tsunamis can lay waste to entire regions. Water erodes foundations when it's not drained properly and can cause incalculable damage when it freezes.

Most relevant to those of us devoted to maintaining healthy recreational bodies of water are the many less dramatic ways that water can cause harm. From waterborne pathogens to disinfection by-products to a spectrum of potentially harmful contaminants, improperly maintained water can make us deathly ill, or worse.

I find it fascinating that the good and bad of water come together in the most intimate of ways in commercial or otherwise public aquatic settings. Think about it, when the water is well-maintained (that is, properly sanitized, oxidized, balanced, and filtered), aquatic facilities become havens of fun, relaxation, therapy, and exercise. Well-maintained aquatic facilities are among the most dynamic and beneficial properties found anywhere in society.

However, if you take that same well-maintained vessel and replace the healthy water with a solution loaded with pathogens, organic compounds, and dissolved solids, all of a sudden the entire scene changes. Where health and fun should rule the day, instead we find discomfort, illness, dysfunction, and even death.

People responsible for recreational and therapeutic bodies of water decide which set of experiences their customers, clients, and constituents will have. We are very much the people who control this profound tipping point between water that is life giving and fluid that is life threatening. It's a heady responsibility, to be sure, but it's also a choice those of us in this profession make with every water treatment and manage decision.

For builders, driving the tipping point means selecting treatment systems that will handle the bather load, along with filtration, hydraulic and control systems that support healthy function. For service technicians, it means establishing effective maintenance and cleaning regimens and troubleshooting problems as they arise. For property owners and managers, it means having the wherewithal and foresight to make the right decisions for your customers and staff.

To my mind, straddling that tipping point is what makes our chosen profession so exciting and also so massively important. Ultimately, we decide which way the aquatic experience goes and when you look at it that way, the choice should be obvious.

Conducting Control

Controlling the many variables that impact recreational water stands as the prime objective for the water quality professional. That may seem an obvious statement, but it's also much easier said than done. Issues with water balance, filtration, sanitation, disinfection by-products, water-related illnesses, organic contaminants, and, ultimately, bather load all conspire to make the job of creating what I call "resilient water" so steep.

Certainly the first step in meeting that challenge is developing a working knowledge of water chemistry, a huge topic that for many of us can take years of experience and study to fully grasp. The second part of the challenge is all about developing and deploying systems that enable the highest possible level of monitoring and control, all of which takes place instantaneously. After all, water problems take form in real time, which means we need to be able to respond with both speed and precision.

In many ways, that capability is what separates the true

professionals from those clinging to increasingly outdated methods.

We've Come a Long Way

Some reading this may say that we have already come a long way in automation and control, and that's perfectly true. There's no question that long-standing technology (including chlorine feeders, ORP and pH controllers, ozone and UV systems, automatic filtration backwashing, and efficient heating systems) have all made water maintenance far easier than it once was.

There are control systems available from multiple manufacturers, and most recently the National Swimming Pool Foundation introduced a control app it developed with the brilliant professionals at Counsilman-Hunsaker. I applaud all of those efforts and encourage professionals striving for greater water quality and system function to do their own research into which systems make the most sense for their businesses.

Yet, for all of those great efforts and innovations, we also know that many facilities, especially high-use commercial aquatic centers, still limp along with systems that cannot keep up with bather loads and all the contaminants that humans introduce to the water. The fact that so many pools have problematic water conditions is evidence that we collectively need to do better.

The "New" App: Remote System Monitoring

I personally believe the solutions can be found in today's ever-advancing control technology, and that's especially true of those systems that enable remote system monitoring. The movement toward "apps" now enables us to monitor and manipulate system functions at multiple sites simultaneously and continuously, and most importantly, respond accordingly. That's a true game changer, even though it might seem as though that technology has been around for quite a while. The fact is those applications are continuing to develop both in capability and in market penetration.

My own experience with offsite control technology began several years ago on a commercial pool where we used versions of Pentair's IntelliTouch and IntelliChem systems. These are outstanding systems that enable you to monitor many pools from one screen remotely, and they deliver the added benefit of email and text alerts. All the systems have protocol adapters that will report to the one main screen allowing you to monitor up to 100 pools on one screen.

The upshot is you can have a broad overview of all the pools with detailed information and helpful data. Also, each site has a history log that allows you to drill down to fine-tune the system and dosing style. You can export system information to an Excel sheet that has data for up to three months for careful analysis. The other great thing is that all the pumps tie into the system allowing control over the pumps' gpm/rpm as well as ability to see wattage/amperage draw, which we use to determine filter backwashing needs.

It's a great system, as are similar systems from other manufacturers, but I personally believe there's still another level we should be looking to achieve.

Looking to the Future

I am currently working with a company outside the industry

that builds control systems for "smart cities" around the country. In meetings with their staff, they have expressed great interest in working with our company, and indeed our industry, to advance water maintenance and security. Basically, they set up command centers where a wide range of security and infrastructure systems are monitored from a central location by a variety of technical means, including video and remote sensor monitoring.

If that level of sophistication were to be applied to the aquatics industry, we could create a class of service professionals that work in a way that's far closer to that of a symphony conductor than a glorified janitor. For people charged with maintaining multiple bodies of high-use water, this type of control is the surest path to avoiding bad water quality and facility downtime.

We are currently working to pair aquatic process instruments to a platform that will enable us to monitor and control multiple locations and a comprehensive set of chemical constituents and system functions. Where this differs from other pool control systems is a range of factors we want to target. It's quite a list that includes water temperature, calcium hardness, flow rate, filter pressure, and much, much more.

Those systems can also provide history data that can be used for analysis and study whenever needed. I also like the idea that such a system can also provide Skype-like video connections that operators can use to discuss issues directly with on-site staff.

That's all obviously a tall order and without doubt, not every system would require monitoring and controlling of all those functions. Still, when you look at the control technology that's being used outside our industry, it's not at all unrealistic to think that we can have systems that monitor and control everything we need and do it instantly from anywhere.

The Experience Factor

When you break it all down, aquatic professionals of all types are ultimately selling the aquatic experience, which includes a variety of enjoyable and beneficial aspects. It's the experience of recreation, health, aesthetic beauty, architectural art, pride of ownership, and togetherness with family and friends. We're selling nothing less than the joy of summer, the thrill of fitness, and cherished memories of family.

Whether it's a small portable spa, residential pool, or a commercial aquatics center, consumers are always buying some variant or combination of those experiences.

But there are several levels to the experience factor, all of which speak to what we as a company are selling; what sets us apart from others in the business — and that is all about the experience of ease and convenience. Over the years, we've developed methods and the application of technology to bring the benefits of aquatic ownership to our customers with the greatest level of convenience, control, comfort, and efficiency. In that sense, we are selling the experience of elevated expectations.

It is a crucial aspect of what we do because part of the ownership experience is the challenge of maintenance. It's perhaps the biggest knock against pools and spas — the fact that all bodies of water require careful and consistent care. Otherwise, all of those primary benefits of aquatic ownership mentioned above are replaced with the burden and abiding negativity of having to spend inordinate time and money taking care of the darn thing. And that's something nobody, in truth, wants to do.

The Hassle Factor

I know this because as someone who is passionate about water treatment and someone who has devoted most of his career to mastering it, even I can't stand the hassle of water testing, calculating dosages, adding the chemicals, and then rechecking the water to make sure it all worked. Fact is, servicing pools is a genuine drag on homeowner enthusiasm, and it is not all that much fun for us professionals either.

What people really want, I'm convinced, is to be able to forget about their pools except for knowing that every time they go to use them, the water will be in perfect condition. They want to have their expectations for the luxury, pleasure, and invigoration associated with getting in the water to be met in full all the time, each and every time.

In saying all this, I realize that achieving a maintenance-free system is a tall order, even one that many people have deemed impossible. All bodies of water require maintenance, which is true, and that hard fact is the mountain those of us in the business seek to climb. Some might even say working to achieve the experience of ultimate convenience is something of a fool's errand, a quixotic quest, of sorts, the impossible dream.

Finding the Solution

The good news is that we now have technology that when deployed in the right set of ways, can, in fact, make for pool and spa operation that is very close to maintenance free. It requires a combination of testing, monitoring, and control technologies that have been with us for quite a long time now. But it's how those modern marvels are applied that gets us and our clients where we hope to go — to a place of convenient experience.

For our company, that approach is represented by our own brand of treatment system, known as HydroZone 3™. It's a "smart pool" system that uses different types of electronic data collection sensors to supply information, which is then used to manage assets and resources efficiently, all from remote locations. The system and the pools themselves are designed to create consistent water quality, safety, and, ultimately, the experience our clients seek.

HydroZone 3 includes automatic oxidation, sanitation, water balance, and control of filter cycles, as well as features such as automatic pool covers. It provides constant chemistry testing, reporting and logging, interface with smartphones, pads, and personal computers. It controls pump speed, heaters, and lights, all of which work to provide professional oversight and response when needed.

Practicing what I preach, I use a HydroZone 3 on my personal hot tub and pool — it's amazing how the system is always several steps ahead of me. I truly believe it's smarter than I am. No human being can constantly monitor any body of water. It's impossible. Now we have a system that does that for you, making programmable adjustments and heading off trouble before it starts.

Ultimately, that's what control technology does, it responds in real time and enables us to address issues before they turn into big problems. When it comes to maintaining resilient water quality, that constancy of control not only provides ultimate convenience, but it also ensures ultimate consumer satisfaction.

That's what the selling experience is all about!

Why HydroZone 3™?

Let's switch gears here and turn to some set of more technical discussions that support the mission and philosophy described in the previous sections.

As described in the previous chapter, my approach to water treatment is embodied in a set of synergistic technologies I've branded as the HydroZone 3 water-treatment system, which I explain throughout this book in several different contexts. The big idea behind the system has been to create an approach that meets the needs of the future, to earnestly advance the state of the art in water quality management.

In short, I believe this system, or more accurately, combination of systems, is the best way to consistently achieve perfect water quality in a pool or spa. No other treatment method comes anywhere close to delivering this level of bather experience.

We created HydroZone 3 a decade ago in an effort to far

exceed minimum water quality guidelines and instead establish the aquatic industry's only true platinum standard. It is, quite simply, the Ferrari or Bentley of water treatment and management systems. The result has been a signature level of water quality that is mesmerizing in its beauty and pristine clarity, the paramount expression of recreational water quality.

That's why these technological wonders have been installed for discerning homeowners and commercial pool owners who expect and demand the greatest value for their investment. It's a bold and beautiful concept that has elevated the way many people think about water quality.

So what exactly is a HydroZone 3 pool?

In a word, it's a "synergistic system" rather than a single chemical product or piece of equipment. The result of years of research and trial and error, HydroZone 3 starts with a carefully balanced combination of corona-discharge ozone generation, medium-pressure UV sterilization and a tiny .5 parts-per-million chlorine residual. (In some cases, we've been able to eliminate chlorine altogether.)

A HydroZone 3 pool is also designed with robust filtration, rapid turnover and skimming action, energy-efficient circulation and uniform chemical distribution. It's a holistic water-management concept that includes advanced monitoring and automation technology, proper materials selection and ergonomic design, all of which work together to maximize convenience, comfort, and efficiency.

Each HydroZone 3 pool is engineered separately to suit the

client's lifestyle, type of use, and desired water temperature. These systems deliver water that requires minimal maintenance with no downtime, all while maintaining perfect mineral balance and easily handling the sanitizer and oxidizer demand, regardless of how many people take a dip or how often. It eliminates all chemical odors, ensures perfect water clarity, and gives water a luxurious texture and pristine cleanliness found nowhere else. These are both the most hygienic and enjoyable pools ever created, bar none!

In other words, HydroZone 3 is all about delivering the finest aquatic experience available anywhere. No, it is not the least expensive option, and may not be for everyone, but for those seeking perfect water quality each and every time they use their pool or spa, this is the only guaranteed way to achieve that level of perfection.

Anything else is a compromise.

As we move along through this text, you'll find detailed explanations of "why" I decided to focus and develop the various different aspects of HydroZone 3. In many ways, it's my greatest recipe, at least since I met water.

(I acknowledge that the above may sound like a sales pitch, and if so, guilty as charged. But it all also happens to be verifiably true.)

Why Ozone?

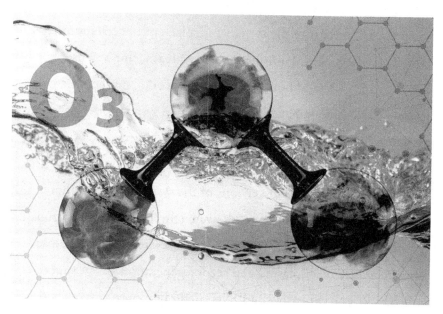

At the heart of the HydroZone 3 system, you'll find ozone.

If you look at the original plans for many commercial aquatic facilities, it's surprising the number of them that were designed with plumbing and electrical systems meant to accommodate ozone systems. Yet, many never had those systems installed. Likewise, when I talk to facility managers and pool operators, they may know some things about ozone but are simply not interested.

That's all part of why, for years now, I've believed that ozone, the almighty O3, one of the most powerful oxidizers known to science, has been one of our most underused and misunderstood methods of water treatment.

Ozone systems designed for treating recreational water have been around for decades. We know about the technology; in fact, most of us in the industry could probably even recite a familiar litany of benefits. Yet, the technology has always had trouble breaking through both with professionals and our clients. The reasons vary; for some it's the cost of the system and a lack of understanding of the return on investment. For others, there's a fear factor because they don't truly understand how ozone systems work, and then there are those who do not appreciate the power these systems offer us in our efforts to ensure superior water quality to our clients.

Truth be told, ozone systems are expensive, they can be tricky to use correctly, and earlier versions of the systems, such as those available back in the early nineties, were temperamental and prone to a handful of common problems. Today's systems, such as those using relatively new "plasma-gap" ozone generation are far superior, but they are still expensive. Still, I contend that once you really delve into the technology, it's easy to see how useful it can be and how ozone might even completely change the way you think about water treatment.

The O3 Revelation

My own journey with ozone technology began about 20 years ago. I was working mostly in service at the time and was in the early stages of my understanding of water chemistry. Similar to others in the profession, I spent many frustrating days chasing changes in chemistry in what often felt like a futile attempt to stabilize my pools in terms of all the issues that go along with what I now view as unstable or non-resilient water treatment. It was like constantly chasing a yo-yo.

That all changed when Del Ozone offered me a free system if I agreed to provide them with three months of daily water test readings as part of a beta testing program. I found a client who liked the idea of getting a system at a dramatically reduced price and he agreed to let me have at it with the daily monitoring routine. In a very short time, I became a true believer. As I recall, it was a five-gram per hour system, which has a relatively low output by today's standards, but, nonetheless, I was blown away by the results.

Almost from day one, the water quality, clarity, look, and feel was nothing like I had ever seen. It was amazing just from a purely subjective view. More impressive still was what I found with the testing. Ozone effectively reduced chlorine consumption by 75 percent, which means you're not forming disinfection by-products at nearly the rate typically associated with traditional halogen disinfection. It didn't impact water balance because ozone has no effect on pH, calcium hardness, or total alkalinity. It doesn't add to the total dissolved solids (TDS) because, ultimately, it's really just an unstable form of oxygen that turns into O2 after it does its work. And best of all, it was always there to oxidize organic compounds.

An Elegant Solution

Overall, it just seemed like a better and more elegant answer to a range of water treatment challenges. And, all of those early observations have been reinforced time and time again over the years, especially as I've grown in my understanding of how it's used. I've found that a properly functioning system — meaning you have it installed correctly and the flow rates and dosages are dialed in — will always be there to oxidize all the organic matter that enters the water via bathers or environmental conditions. It consumes the bad stuff and leaves you with beautiful water quality.

There are nuances that I'm still figuring out to this day. For example, there's a balance between contact time and dosage. Is it better to use a lower dosage with longer contact times or vice versa? Nowadays, we set up our contact tanks so the flow rate can be adjusted (always keeping in mind we're shooting for treating 25 percent of the overall flow in the ozone bypass) and the output of many of today's systems are self-adjusting. If, for example, the oxidation reduction potential (ORP) drops below 300 millivolts, the system will ramp up to bring the level back to the desired level of 750 or greater.

Seeing and Believing

What we've found is that if clients see what kind of water quality they can have, most of them go for it. These days, 90 percent of our new construction projects include ozone and UV. As for service clients, a majority will also opt for the system once they've tried it on a trial basis. Even if they don't completely understand how it works, the water speaks for itself.

Over and over again, I've seen ozone installed on existing pools, and within 12 hours of turning on the system, the water takes on a distinctly improved quality. It sparkles, there's a shimmer and clarity that impresses most anyone who sees the improvement. It's particularly great in indoor pools, both residential and commercial, where the pungent odor of chloramines, the infamous "chlorine smell," is replaced by a fresh scent in the air. The entire environment just feels cleaner.

Much of all that is very hard to quantify, which I'm sure is also part of why this wonderful technology has been slow in acceptance, at least in our industry. By contrast, ozone treatment has been widely and successfully adopted by agriculture, food processing, manufacturing, laboratory settings, and municipal water treatment among other places, and in many cases for much the same set of reasons that I became an ozone advocate over two decades ago.

To be clear, I do not see ozone as the only solution to all water chemistry challenges because there are so many other components, for example, water balance, filtration, circulation, and sanitization. Also, because it's such a powerful tool, it's crucial that the professionals who specify ozone as well as install and maintain the systems know what they're doing. As the old saying goes, "It's not the tool, it's the mechanic."

Indeed, the most important variable in the entire water treatment equation is the know-how of the professional. To that final and most important point, the main reason I'm so in favor of ozone technology is precisely because I took the time to learn about it. If you stay on the sidelines and only ever learn the most basic aspects of ozone, it will always remain somewhat mysterious. Once you pull back the curtain, however, you will find a number of reasons why ozone might just be right for you and your clients.

Why UV?

Ultraviolet (UV) water treatment is both an exciting and somewhat mysterious way to sanitize water. In recent years, it's become widely used in treating swimming pool water because it's been proven an effective way to control pathogens without adding any chemicals to the water whatsoever.

It also offers other benefits such as destroying chloramines and controlling ozone off gassing by turning it into hydroxyl radicals through the even more mysterious set of chemical reactions collectively known as "advanced oxidation process."

For those reasons, UV has become a key component in our company's approach to ensuring superior water quality for our clients. Like all the treatment methods we use, UV doesn't offer all the answers, but it does play a role in meticulous water treatment.

I first learned about UV back in 2002 when my son and I visited the Mystic Sea Aquarium in Mystic, Connecticut. I've always loved aquariums and have long been interested in how they keep the waters clear while harboring all those fish and other sea creatures. (Talk about "bather load"—aquariums maintain clear water while serving as full-time homes for scores if not hundreds of animals. That's impressive to say the least.)

UV and Ponds and Aquariums

At one of the tanks while my son was marveling at the fish, I noticed columns of bubbles that I immediately gathered were part of the treatment scheme, not unlike the way home aquariums are oxygenated with bubblers. Off to the side I noticed a box with all these tubes feeding into it. I didn't know what it was, but I immediately recognized the company name emblazoned on the side, "Pentair." Given that's a brand I associate with swimming pool equipment, I couldn't help but wonder what kind of Pentair product was being used on a large-scale aquarium.

Turns out, it was a UV system. That spurred my interest, and I soon delved into what UV was all about. There's quite a lot to understanding the technology but long story short, back in those days it was a treatment method largely associated with managing water in ponds as well as aquariums.

That all made sense because in those "naturalistic" systems, the idea is to treat water without using halogens, such as chlorine, because it will kill fish and plants. As it happened, back then UV was starting to also be used on swimming pools because of its effective way of stunting the growth of pathogens, which proponents of the technology point out is a great way to reduce chlorine consumption in pools.

And although UV does not provide any kind of sanitizing residual or oxidize anything, for many professionals, its work on harmful microorganisms justifies the expense of installing it on pools and even some spas.

I began experimenting with the technology and quickly recognized how when combined with other treatment methods, it could dramatically improve water quality. I understood from the start, however, that it is not a stand-alone treatment method.

A Natural Companion

It can be tricky to explain how UV works. I've seen many descriptions, and this one from evoqua.com explains it as well as any I've found:

Ultraviolet (UV) light is energy within the electromagnetic spectrum that has shorter wavelengths than that which are visible to the human eye. UV light is a range of electromagnetic waves from 100 to 400 nanometers (between x-ray and visible light). The division of UV light is classified as Vacuum UV (100-200 nm), UV-C (200-280 nm), UV-B (280-315 nm) and UV-A (315-400 nm). The energy waves provided in the UV-C spectrum demonstrate the germicidal efficiencies that provide highly effective disinfection.

To be perfectly honest, all these years later I'm still working to fully understand the nuances of UV treatment, but through extensive practical evaluation and lots of trial and error, we have learned to apply UV to our treatment systems in a way that serves as a perfect complement to our ozone and chlorine treatment systems.

I do know that UV kills pathogens not by lysing them the way chlorine or other oxidizers do, but instead by scrambling their DNA so they can't reproduce. UV has long been proven effective in reducing pathogen numbers to harmless levels when used properly.

In the HydroZone 3 system, we create a bypass loop that uses an ozone generator and a contact tank to treat 25 percent of the circulation. For that 25 percent, ozone does an amazing job of oxidizing organic compounds and killing microorganisms. The remaining 75 percent is sanitized using UV, which is installed downstream of the ozone bypass. (In our systems, ozone handles the lion's share of oxidation, while UV handles the sanitizing.)

UV also has the added benefit of destroying excess ozone before it re-enters the pool, which has major implications for indoor pools, especially where ozone off gassing can be dangerous and is prohibited.

In other words, the two technologies complement each other. Neither would be nearly as effective without the other. UV is a perfect role player — and that's why SRK Modern Pool Solutions uses UV!

Why Chlorine?

For more than 100 years, chlorine has been the primary chemical used to treat swimming pool water and public drinking water. It remains in widespread use in spite of the fact that it has stiff competition from so-called alternative sanitizers.

For all of its water treatment supremacy and long-time use, chlorine remains badly misunderstood. To a large extent, it has been maligned, even demonized, and that's really too bad. The reason for the negativity surrounding chlorine is, I believe, due to the way it's been misused and over used.

The Good and the Bad

The ills associated with chlorine are familiar and have almost become a mantra for those who seek to eliminate it altogether. It's harsh on skin, eyes, hair, and bathing suits; it smells; it's highly corrosive; it forms disinfection by-products; and it can be rendered almost useless at high pH and in pools with elevated cyanuric acid levels.

Truth be told, most of those issues — particularly the smell as well as skin and eye irritation — are the result of disinfection by-products such as chloramines, which form when free available chlorine oxidizes compounds containing ammonia and nitrogen. The fact that it's pH sensitive is only a problem in pools with improper water balance. Plus, its complex relationship with cyanuric acid, a UV (from sunlight) stabilizer, only becomes an issue if you let the cyanuric acid level climb too high.

Nonetheless, the dark side of chlorine has given rise to an ethos that says less is more and none is even better. Still, there are reasons why chlorine has stuck around in spite of the negative perception. It's both an effective oxidizer and sanitizer, it stays in solution, and it can be stabilized in sunlight, which other sanitizers such as bromine and biguanides cannot. No other chemical I know combines all those upsides.

A Layer of Protection

The problems associated with chlorine occur when it's used as a solo act. When used alone, the recommended 1-to-3 parts per million (ppm) in a residential pool and 3-to-5 ppm in a commercial pool are, indeed, problematic. First of all, even when you're using a feeder and/or an oxidation reduction potential (ORP) controller, the level of free available chlorine, hypochlorous acid, will fluctuate due to chlorine demand courtesy of bathers and other environmental factors. At those residual levels, there's a lot of chlorine in the water that will combine with organic compounds and form the unwanted by-products and particularly trichloramine, which causes the chlorine smell.

That all points to a simple remedy: keep the residuals down. That's one of the many reasons our preferred treatment method involves ozone, UV, and chlorine. In our HydroZone3 system we maintain a small 0.6-ppm chlorine level to kill any bacteria that develops in the pool itself before the water has had a chance to circulate through the UV and ozone systems.

In other words, the chlorine plays a limited role yet offers a very necessary measure of protection.

The Many Flavors of Chlorine

Prior to developing our system, I was like many, many other service technicians, driving around with a huge amount of liquid bleach in my truck, which is expensive and to an extent, somewhat hazardous. I was constantly testing and adding chlorine to keep up with the demand, which was almost impossible in high-use pools. When the combined chlorine, i.e., by-products, developed or the pool had an algae bloom, I'd turn to either chlorine or non-chlorine shock, which requires adding huge amounts of chemicals to reach what chemists call "breakpoint chlorination."

Using chlorine as the one and only sanitizer was like living on the proverbial hamster wheel. It felt like a futile pain in the backside.

Chlorine is sold in many forms and over the years, I have tried them all. And all that experience taught me that each type of chlorine has different characteristics and using each correctly means selecting the right type for the application at hand. To sum up, you have to understand the specific characteristics of the chlorine you're using. Some types dissolve very slowly and others more quickly. Some perform better in hot water than others.

These days, I really like using cal-hypo tablets because they're very slow dissolving, which means it's easy to control the residual level. It also adds calcium, which in many areas is a plus because of low levels of calcium in the tap water.

Overall, I've found that when you use chlorine in a sparing way, the problems associated with it essentially vanish. Using less also saves money, which contributes to the return on investment for the other systems we use.

That's why I believe the objective shouldn't be to eliminate chlorine, but instead to use it in the best possible way.

Advanced Oxidation Process

For the past few years, the aquatics industry has adopted a new concept known as AOP (advanced oxidation processes). The term, which was first coined in 1987 by research scientist William Glaze, refers to a set of chemical reactions that produce a chemical species known as hydroxyl radicals (OH) or sometimes incorrectly referred to as nascent oxygen.

Hydroxyl radicals are one of the most powerful oxidizers known to science, capable of oxidizing almost any organic compound. The catch is that in water they exist in solution for only a very tiny fraction of a second, so short-lived, in fact, there is no way to test for them and to a large extent their very existence requires what amounts to a theoretical assumption.

Hydroxyl radicals occur naturally in the atmosphere and have long been considered "nature's scrub brush" because of the way they in effect clean the air we breathe. In water treatment, AOPs are artificially achieved by providing a primary oxidative resource, either ozone, hydrogen peroxide, or dissolved oxygen, combined with an energy resource, typically UV light or in some cases a catalyst such as titanium dioxide. Once the hydroxyl radical is formed, it reacts almost instantaneously with any organic compound it comes in contact with, which is "mineralized" to non-organic compounds such as water, carbon dioxide, and various salts.

Although scientists have been studying these complex chemical reaction for decades, and especially so since the term was coined, AOP technology has been slowly adapted in wastewater treatment and only by a handful of companies in the pool and spa industry. It is now recognized by most chemistry experts and is one of the main reasons that in the MAHC (Model Aquatic Health Code) the CDC recommends a "secondary" pillar of sanitization using ozone and UV in order to produce supplemental AOPs in commercial pools and spas.

While the hard science is established in terms of many of the chemical reactions of how hydroxyl radicals are formed and the way they mineralize organic compounds, there remains a number of aspects of AOP that is still unknown, most of which are based on purely subjective analysis of water quality.

Feeling is Believing

I've personally been working with AOP systems for about a decade now. My approach is to ozonate water and then treat it with UV light, which in turn transforms some of the ozone into hydroxyl radicals. This has a dual benefit. First, by treating the ozonated water with UV light, the ozone is in effect destroyed and does not enter the pool, which of course prevents injury and damage that can result from high levels of dissolved ozone, which can remain in solution for 18 minutes.

Secondly, by forming hydroxyl radicals, the water is cleansed of nearly all of the organic compounds present, which in turn reduces demand on the low levels of chlorine we use. It also eliminates any disinfection by-products and obliterates any nutrient source for pathogens and algae.

As I've mentioned earlier, I've done a great deal of personal experimentation with these processes in my own spa at home, which I use for my daily soaking and hydrotherapy ritual I affectionately refer to as my "Daily U." Through these ongoing observations, I've learned that this combination of ozone and UV and the resulting AOP provide a level of water quality that is nothing short of phenomenal. It has a silky quality and level of pristine cleanliness I've never experienced any other way.

In fact, I'll go so far as to say that the sensation associated with soaking in this water is the kind of experience that can only be described in highly subjective almost spiritual terms. It is water that in my experience becomes remarkably rejuvenating and healing and that reaches the highest possible level of hydrotherapy.

As I've played with the process by comparing the results with the UV system on and off, I've run into some surprisingly consistent results. When the UV is not running, the water quality changes. While it's still clean and clear, but it takes on an entirely different characteristic. It has a bite or sharpness to it, sort of like the crisp flavor of Coca-Cola. You can feel it in your eyes and on your skin.

I assume this is due to the ozone that is not being turned into hydroxyl radical. In practical applications, we can measure the ORP (oxidative reduction potential) generated when the UV is running or not. Because it changes the ozone into the incredibly short-lived hydroxyl radical, the difference is reflected in a drop in ORP. That's where things get somewhat confusing for a lot of people, because it's counterintuitive to think of a drop in ORP as a good thing, but in this case, it means that the ozone is being transformed into the highly reactive hydroxyl radical that is in turn oxidizing the organics in the water. Because hydroxyl radicals exist only for a few thousandths of a second, they are not measured as part of ORP.

Noticeable Difference

When I've run my informal experiments with my kids and a handful of my clients, it's amazing how attuned they become to the difference in water quality. When the UV system is off, I immediately get comments about how the water just doesn't feel quite as nice, just as I've experienced. When it's turned back on, those comments immediately change from complaints to nothing but high praise for the way the water makes them feel. The only difference is the presence or lack of the hydroxyl radicals. It's come to the point that my kids can jump in and immediately tell whether the UV system is on or off. They'll yell, "Dad, UV off!" And, they've been right every single time.

How exactly it is that hydroxyl radicals make such a huge difference in the feel of the water remains unknown. We do know quite a lot about the chemical reactions it drives when it's formed and then subsequently makes such blindingly quick work of organic compounds, but why exactly it so dramatically impacts the aesthetic experience, we do not now, nor may ever know for sure.

To my way of thinking, we should be comfortable with those mysteries because there is no question about the water quality AOP supports. As the technology becomes more widespread in public water treatment, industrial and laboratory applications, as well as in pools and spas, it's very likely that we'll find out more and more about the amazing advantages of AOP.

For now, I contend we really shouldn't need any more proof to know that this amazing set of chemical processes will be a part of artisan water treatment from this point forward. Those who adapt AOP generation will be on the cutting edge of providing superior aquatic experiences to their clients, those who don't will likely fall far behind in those efforts. When we consider the future of aquatics, it's obvious that story will be written with the letters, A, O, and P.

Building and Designing for Water Quality

Now, let's return to the subject of setting up a pool for success.

A well-designed, installed, and maintained pool can truly be a thing of beauty. So much so it's not surprising at all that homeowners and property owners tend to concentrate on aesthetics when they're in the planning stages of purchasing a new pool or remodeling an old one. We humans are, after all, visual creatures by nature and we like pretty things.

The only problem is that the pool's shape, plaster color, and type of coping as well as fire features, beach entries, and expensive tile mosaics are all for not if the water itself isn't clean, clear, and sparkling. Great water makes visually average pools more appealing, and pools with exciting visual designs even more so. It's the water that brings the shimmer regardless of the vessel that contains it, and it's the water that will mire the most beautiful of designs when poorly maintained. That's why I think that many builders have it backwards when it comes to design and engineering. Instead of focusing entirely on aesthetics, shouldn't the needs of the pool be considered first? Make no mistake, I love great design and architecture as much as anyone, but leaving water quality to an afterthought, as many unfortunately do, undercuts the whole point of owning a pool or spa in the first place.

Yes, chemical treatment is a major part of it but so are filtration, skimming, pipe size, returns, flow rates, and a host of other factors. The first questions we should be asking are: what's the anticipated bather load and frequency of use, the desired water temperature, are there trees and other plants that will add debris to the water, are there dogs likely to use the pool, are birds an issue? All of those and other questions about use and the environment drive decisions we make about how to treat the water and configure the system.

On the Surface

As both a service technician and a builder, I've come to understand a number of specifics about how you should build a pool so that it's both easy to maintain and will consistently provide top-shelf water quality. For example, one of the most important of those lessons is all about skimming; that is, removing that top half-inch of water as quickly and efficiently as possible.

When it comes to contaminants, the surface is where the action is. Common sense dictates that all debris and environmental pollutants first enter the surface of the water and experience servicing.

Using pools and spas has taught me that the stuff that humans add, and I'll spare listing those, mostly floats on the surface. Therefore, it holds that if you can skim the surface and treat it quickly, a host of water quality problems will be either dramatically reduced or avoided altogether.

It's not surprising that many of the problem pools I've serviced were those with inadequate skimmers. In designing pools for water quality, I've found that sometimes it's best to overshoot the skimming action. If that design calls for 10 skimmers, I might switch gears and suggest going with vanishing edges or perimeter overflows, also known as the Lautner Edge.

Like so many aspects of pool design and engineering, making adjustments before you break ground is far better than trying to fix things when they're literally set in concrete. (More on skimmers later.)

Every Aspect of Design

Much the same holds true with returns. If you distribute returns in a smart way, such as across the bottom of the pool, you'll achieve more effective chemical distribution and in heated pools, make far more efficient use of the Btus (British thermal units).

Likewise, you can't say enough about the importance of proper filtration. I'm a big fan of sand filters, but whatever filtration you use; ensuring proper flow rates and filter area are paramount in designing for great water quality.

To that end, proper plumbing size is another critical factor, precisely because it is a key factor in the hydraulic design, increasing the efficiency of all the system components, from the pumps to the heaters to the filters to the chemical treatment systems. It's a common refrain that's been repeated many times, but for good reason: undersized plumbing and oversized pumps waste energy and create an imbalanced system that compromises all aspects of pool and spa operation.

And, of course, as I've discussed many times, multi-layered chemical treatment driven by advanced control systems brings it all together.

Each of these factors could serve as the subject of extensive discussions and often are in seminar rooms and industry publications and websites, but the overriding point is that it only makes sense to think about the most important element in pools and spas first when it comes to designing and engineering — and that important element is always the water.

Critical Construction

Sometimes in order to understand how to do things right, it can be helpful to examine what happens when something goes terrible wrong. As an example, our company worked on a renovation project that offered a dramatic example of what can happen when a pool builder doesn't know what they're doing and/or tries to cut corners to keep their price down while padding the bottom line.

Unfortunately, it's a common scenario in our industry, which has earned the dubious reputation of being full of jackals and thieves who essentially lie to unsuspecting homeowners to land their business. I've come to expect that companies such as ours, those that never take short cuts but instead earn our bread by delivering value for the dollar, are often left out in the cold simply because many homeowners are shopping based entirely on the price tag.

This is why we cherish those clients who ask questions and seek to understand in greater detail what exactly it is that they're buying. It's a sad state of affairs that our customers can't simply rely on the word of people in our industry to deliver what they promise, but that's the way it stands. The more clients know about what it takes to properly design, engineer, and construct a swimming pool, the more likely they are to make a decision based on long-term value rather than upfront cost.

Unfortunately, that's not what happened in this case. A general contractor who was using another pool builder sold the unwitting client the proverbial bill of goods and the results were horrendous. In this case, the GC led the client to believe that our company was the one doing the work, when in fact our bid had been rejected in favor of the much lower bid by the GC. The pool builder that did do the work, did everything as cheaply as possible and was rewarded with huge profits.

So, here's what went wrong and more important a list of basic pool construction issues/questions that would have saved the client untold grief and expense.

Bad on Bad

First, the pool wasn't built to handle the client's lifestyle. She wanted 95-degree pool water and the system simple wasn't able to generate the kind of heat rise or turnover required for that kind of spa-like temperature. In a nutshell, it needed a turnover rate five times greater than what it had. With temperatures like that you need to work to therapy pool standards, which have turnover rates of three hours. This pool wasn't remotely close to that standard, although the homeowner was led to believe otherwise.

That's bad enough, but amazingly only the smaller of the two major problems. The second and by far more serious issue was that the pool was built on uncompacted fill and was not engineered for the soil conditions. It was a classic case of the builder saying that he had worked in the area for decades and didn't need a soils report. The result was a pool structure that had no type of foundation that would anchor the pool to competent load-bearing soil or bedrock. It was a concrete shell basically just floating in loose material — and, not surprising, almost immediately the shell started to move.

The deep end started to rise out of the ground and the shallow end moved lower, so among other problems, the vanishing edge wasn't spilling properly. In fact, the edge never worked. Then during the winter the deep end settled and the shallow end started to rise, that's when the pool shell basically cracked in half. It moved around so much that it was like the pool was almost alive. The weir wall was cracking, the coping was cracking, the pool leaked like a sieve, and you had to basically add water constantly just to keep it full. Suffice to say it was a service nightmare and completely unacceptable on all levels.

We became involved when the homeowner got in touch with us directly thinking that we had built the pool. Suffice to say, the client was outraged upon discovering that we, in fact, had nothing to do with the pool's construction. Still, we came on the scene and started trying to do what we could to help. But the pool was riddled with so many issues that over time, the client decided to rip the whole thing out and have our company rebuild it from scratch.

We've since discovered just how badly this pool was botched.

Not only did it not have a foundation and was built in what engineers have since determined is completely unbuildable soil, the builder used rebound in several places, shot the pool directly against the ground, which in this case was completely unsuitable as a "form" for the pool shell, there were all sorts of shadowing that left gaps in the shell and the compression strength of the concrete was almost non-existent, well below 2,000 psi. It was about as bad as bad gets.

The result is that we removed the first pool entirely and replaced it with one that was designed and engineered properly. And, it cost roughly three times the original price of the pool. We installed a system that will heat and turn over the water in less than three hours with multiple returns and balanced plumbing loops. The treatment systems will provide excellent water quality and we used an unusual foundation scheme where the equipment room is below the pool and acts as the structural support, all engineered based on the soil conditions.

There's little question the client will be seeking damages in a civil suit, but in the meantime, she's been subjected to a horrible

This mess could've been avoided with attention to construction basics.

experience that is about as far removed from what she wanted originally as one could imagine.

Buyers Beware

All of this begs the big question of how to avoid this kind of unmitigated catastrophe. Here's a short list of some of the distinctions that set us apart from the kind of negligent companies that created the disaster described above. We'll stick with just the structural issues for this discussion as simple examples. These points would easily become part of a list of questions that a reasonably informed homeowner might ask a prospective builder.

First, we start with a soils report. It's really just common sense: you have to know the soil conditions you're building in; otherwise, it's absolutely impossible to engineer the shell to last. When you're building a concrete structure in the ground that's meant to hold water, there's no room for guesswork. Soil conditions can vary from property to property and saying that you've worked in the area for a long time and know the conditions without testing just does not cut it.

Next, we build freestanding shells, a huge distinction that sets us apart from many builders. That means we over-excavate the site and we form the pool as though it was going to exist above ground. This enables us to create a precise shell, typically using half-inch rebar, 10 inches on center in the floor and six inches in the walls. We build perfectly vertical walls, which can be next to impossible when you're using the ground as a form.

Our shells are 10 inches thick and engineered to withstand geological forces as well as freeze-thaw conditions. We're able to widen the shell beneath coping as much as three feet extending down below the freeze line. That is so there's no movement during the winter, meaning the coping and tile line won't crack or come loose. Our forms are built sturdy so they there's no movement during the shotcrete application.

We make sure the shotcrete is applied properly, which means we avoid shadowing and we never use rebound. A lot of contractors will use rebound in the steps and the spas, for example, which doesn't even really qualify as concrete, it's more like loose sand and will almost always lead to cracks and other structural defects.

Had the homeowner known about these simple issues, there's a chance she would've been able to ask the right questions that would've enabled her to avoid the trouble and expense that followed.

There's certainly a huge list that goes beyond the structural issues, such as what type of surface, is it traditional plaster or something else such as polished aggregate which is more durable? How is the water being filtered and chemically treated? Is the system run on variable speed pumps? How many skimmers and returns are in the system? What types of lights are being used, LEDs or traditional incandescent or halogen lights? What type of control system is being used? The list goes on and on.

It's a hard and inconvenient fact that consumers need to be educated in order to protect themselves from the kind of thievery that took place on the project described above. Truth is a dose of practical knowledge and the right questions can be critical in helping homeowners see beyond the price.

Why Sand Filtration?

As I've written several times before, I'm a huge proponent of modern water treatment technology. I believe we're seeing developments right now that may have far-reaching impacts on how we manage water quality, both in pools and in public utilities and other applications.

With all those big ideas in mind, it may be a surprise to some that when it comes to the subject of filtration, I fall into the "old-school" category. Specifically, I'm a proponent of using sand filtration as opposed to DE (diatomaceous earth) or cartridges. Here are my reasons why:

First, DE and cartridge filters require ongoing maintenance. DE grids must be cleaned, often repaired or replaced, and the DE itself needs to be handled as toxic waste. Even handling fresh DE is hazardous if it's inhaled. And, frankly, the process of cleaning a DE filter is simply a miserable chore. It's disgusting. It also takes time and energy and adds to the cost of maintaining a pool.

Cartridge filters also require cleaning and eventual replacement. Granted the process is not as objectionable as cleaning a DE filter, but it does require changing out dirty cartridges with clean ones and putting the used units through a careful process of soaking in TSP (tri-sodium phosphate) or another cleaning solution, and then painstakingly cleaning all the pleats. Again, it adds travel, time, and expense to the maintenance process.

Sand Filtration Benefits

Sand is different. It's cleaned by backwashing, often-automatic backwashing and, therefore, does not require much, if any maintenance. If the pool is managed properly, the sand media can last indefinitely.

Second, the backwashing process adds fresh water to the pool and discards a portion of the old. I've long believed, as my friend and pool genius Dave Peterson teaches in his Genesis 3 classes (one of the best educational programs ever in the industry) "the solution to pollution is dilution." It's common sense that replacing worn-out water with clean water is a tool, a layer of treatment that stacks the chemistry deck in our favor by getting rid of a portion of all that TDS (total dissolved solids) that builds up over time.

Some people will counter that backwashing wastes water, which is detrimental in areas impacted by drought. Fair enough. On the conservation end of things, however, I can't help but think that the energy saved by not having to travel to the site and maintenance of the DE or cartridge filters is a big plus from an ecological standpoint.

And finally, what some people will probably find most surprising is that I see the larger filter micron size in sand filters as an advantage over DE and cartridges. Manufacturers of cartridge filters especially have done a great job reducing the micron size down, and DE has always filtered down to a tiny particle size, as well. By contrast, sand filters remove particulates in the 15- to 20-micron range. So how on earth is that better? Don't DE and cartridges make for cleaner water?

If you're using a single-pronged treatment regimen, most typically chlorine, then I would agree, you probably need the small filtration to keep the water clean. But when you have other layers of treatment, such as ozone and UV as we use in our systems, and proper skimming and return circulation with no dead spots, then you don't need to filter down to such a small size. The entire system is working synergistically and the 15-micron level is more than adequate.

Also, those smaller micron sized filters mean that DE and cartridge filters load up far more quickly. When the media gets dirty, you're slowing down the flow rate, which will in turn impact heater function, chemical feeders, and overall hydraulic performance. (As an aside, often when a heater isn't working, as an example, the cause is a dirty DE or cartridge filter.)

Worse yet, dirty media means you're actually adding contaminants back into the water. You wouldn't use a dirty coffee filter to make your morning cup of java; in the same sense, pool water should never pass through media that is loaded with all the material you want to remove in the first place. It's simply counterproductive and deepens the challenge of maintaining a clean pool.

Those are the reasons I prefer the tried-and-true qualities of sand filtration.

Why *NOT* Salt?

When discussing chemical treatment options for pools and spas, I'm often asked about saltwater chlorination. Many people have heard a lot of good things about it and are curious if it's a good choice for them.

I'll come clean right here at the start and say that I am not an advocate of this technology, although I do understand the appeal. "Saltwater pools" have been around a long time and have seen a dramatic rise and, later, fall in popularity. The technology came to the U.S. in the early nineties, originating in Australia. It caught on slowly at first, but then in the early 2000s, it seemed as though everyone wanted to transition to the method.

And make no mistake; saltwater chlorination does come with a considerable list of potential benefits. You don't have to purchase chlorine, transport it, or store it on site. Saltwater pools gained a reputation for silky smooth water, and it is true that the electrolytic process does provide constant super-chlorination inside the salt cell itself, thus constantly breaking up chloramines a little bit at a time.

The problems I saw, however, started with the way the systems were marketed as being maintenance-free and, even more inaccurately, that they're not using chlorine. In fact, salt pools do require tremendous levels of maintenance, and they are most definitely chlorinated; it's just that the chlorine is added in a different way than more traditional methods, such as feeders or the bottle-at-the-end-of-the-arm method.

Giving It a Try

Still, there was a time when I did try the concept with a handful of my service accounts. It was in the practical application that the drawbacks became abundantly clear.

First, there's the issue that you have to add hundreds of pounds of salt to a pool, based on the volume of water, and you have to continue to add salt based on splash out or leaks. It struck me how adding all this salt is a tremendous amount of effort and expense. The wear and tear on the service vehicles hauling around that much salt adds up more quickly than one might expect.

The biggest problem I found was how the method impacts water balance. Adding that much salt increased the pH, as does the chlorine generation process itself, so I needed to add acid to lower the pH, and that, in turn, lowers the alkalinity as well. Then we needed to add more sodium bicarbonate to bring up the alkalinity again. As a result, I was caught in a constant yo-yo effect that aggravates water's natural ability to scale and corrode. It was a nightmare.

A Corrosive Character

Perhaps most troubling of all, saltwater is highly corrosive. The electrolytic properties of dissolved sodium chloride will destroy metal components such as light rings, handrails, and filter internals. The corrosive nature of saltwater will also wreak havoc with certain cementitious or stone materials.

Not surprising, the concept has fallen out of favor with many builders and service technicians, myself included. I went from being at least open-minded about it to now being entirely opposed to using saltwater chlorination on any of our pools.

The Role of Skimmers

There's a yin and yang to the art of building and maintaining pools and spas. On one hand, the chemistry can be fairly complex. I realize that there are many people who make the case that water quality maintenance is not rocket science, which of course is true, but that should not dismiss the fact that there is a lot to it. Water chemistry is constantly shifting and all the parts work together. It's the kind of discipline that you can spend a career studying and refining, but never completely perfect.

On the other hand, there are many aspects of pool and spa "science" that are extremely simple in concept and application. One of the most important, and also the least considered by many people, is the humble skimmer.

Fact is, basically all man-made bodies of water have some form of skimming mechanism. From man-made lakes, to ponds, to commercial pools, to fountains and the smallest spa, they all need skimmers. In fact, skimmers are so common that even some manufacturers that sell them barely say much or promote them at all.

That lack of attention is even more evident on the builder end of the equation where many, if not a majority of pools are built with just one or two skimmers, often with imbalanced or inadequate flow rates. In those systems, it can be extremely difficult to maintain water quality, because the top half-inch of water, which is where most of the contamination and debris exists within any pool, is not being removed.

What I find odd about that disconnect is that it flies in the face of just how important skimmers are to the function of pools and maintaining water quality. It's really just common sense; basically all the stuff that mucks up water enters through the surface, whether it's leaves, dust, bugs, bird crap, or suntan lotion on the bodies of the people entering the pool. Most of that stuff will float long enough so that when you do have adequate skimming action, it can be removed before it sinks. The big stuff gets caught in the skimmer basket, the smaller particles in the filter and all the organic compounds and microorganisms and algae are chemically treated. All those fundamental functions start with the skimmer.

That's why if you're paying attention, it's pretty easy to tell when a pool is lacking adequate skimming action. There will almost inevitably be an oily scum line around the pool. It's easy to ignore if you don't look closely at the surface, but you can feel the oily texture when you put your hand in the water. If you were to somehow compare pools side-by-side, one with proper skimming and one without, you'd notice a dramatic difference in the appearance of the water. But in practice, people grow accustomed to the way their pool looks and it becomes one of those out of sight, out of mind things.

Making it Work

There are a handful of key skimmer considerations that need to be calculated in order to make sure the surface is being removed along with all its contamination. First, you have to have enough skimmers. I see many 20-by-40 pools with two or even just one skimmer. That's not enough. Some might say it's overkill but I wouldn't hesitate to put in six skimmers in that size pool.

There are standards for numbers of skimmers in the Model Aquatic Health Code, one per 500 square feet in a commercial pool but I've always thought those minimum standards are usually not enough, depending on certain variables such as bather load and environmental factors.

But there's more to it than just the number, skimmers also need to be arranged properly to avoid dead spots. That can have a lot to do with the shape of the pool and the location of the returns. For example, when I run skimmers down opposite sides of a rectangular pool, I'll stagger them so that one is essentially skimming a lane or corridor of water across the surface of the pool. For pools with irregular shapes, I'll locate skimmers and returns in areas that will have spots where debris can gather.

Finally, having the specified flow rate through each skimmer is huge. That range is typically anywhere from 30 to 50 gpm. That's simple enough to divide the flow over the number of skimmers to achieve a desired turnover rate for the entire system. The problem is that many pools are plumbed incorrectly and the flow is not evenly distributed among the skimmers. That's especially true when you see skimmers plumbed in sequence, where the first one in line pulls too much water and the subsequent skimmers don't move enough. The right way to plumb skimmers is using a looped trunk line where each one has a balanced flow.

Being Equalized

Another common mistake I see is the absence of an equalizer line and/or an auto fill system. Obviously, skimmers require a given water level to function properly. We also know that there are going to be times when the water level drops, often by simple splash out when a bunch of people jump in the water at the same time. Water loss can also happen by way of excessive evaporation in extremely hot and dry climates or by leaks.

Whatever the cause, when the water drops, skimmers need equalizer lines to continue to pull water into the system. Otherwise, the pump starts to suck air through the dry skimmer, which causes all sorts of problems and damage to equipment. It also helps to have a float valve that closes when the water level drops to further protect against air entering the system via the empty skimmer.

With an auto-fill system, the level will return to normal, but that doesn't happen instantly, so you definitely need the equalizer line to protect the system when the water level is low.

When skimmers are properly incorporated into the original design and construction, all of these issues are easily accommodated at a relatively low cost. When the number, layout, and plumbing of skimmers are not carefully considered, odds are the pool will never function properly and setting the system straight after the fact as part of a remodel is an extremely expensive proposition.

Yes, skimmers may be extremely commonplace, even visually unattractive and certainly easy to take for granted. But understanding why they are so important and how they should be used is one of those fundamentals all water quality professionals should have dialed in from the start.

The Great Cover Up

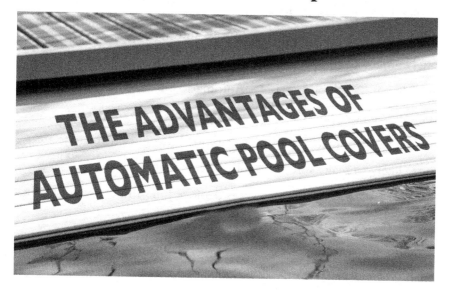

There are a number of features that can add tremendous value to a swimming pool. For example, anyone who's been reading these discussions should know by now that I'm a huge proponent of modern water treatment technology, and equally passionate about proper hydraulics, circulation, filtration, and automated controls. I love LED lights and durable polished aggregate finishes, and I'm a huge fan of subterranean equipment vaults, to name a few of my favorite things.

Another item that's often worth serious consideration is an automatic pool cover. Here in the seasonal climes of the great Northeast, we winterize pools, which obviously means they need to be covered much of the year. There are different types of covers you can use, but for my two cents, none compare to the advantages of the automatic pool cover, for winterizing and year-round.

Safe, Clean and Convenient

The main reason people buy an automatic pool cover is for safety. That's especially true for families with small children who are at the greatest risk of drowning. Automatic pool covers are among the most reliable safety features. First, because they are so easy to use, opening and closing at the touch of a button, homeowners are more likely to make sure the pool is covered when it's not in use. It's a simple fact that when the cover is deployed, it's impossible to fall in the water.

After safety comes a list of some practical advantages covers offer. Chief among them, covers keep debris from falling in the pool. That means in turn the filter doesn't have to work as hard to keep the water clean and you'll inevitably use less chemicals to keep the water safe, clear, and clean.

Also, because the water is kept cleaner, it requires less time and effort to maintain. You don't have to vacuum, net, or brush the pool nearly as often. And, skimmers and pump strainer baskets don't become full as quickly and filters require less frequent cleaning or backwashing. Furthermore, because the pool is clean, it's always ready to use when you open the cover, an advantage that definitely enhances the consumer experience.

Energy savings: this is an advantage most people don't consider when thinking about whether or not to include an auto cover, but it's a big one to be sure. Fact is, the most energy used in a pool comes by way of heat loss due to evaporation. (This is why all portable spas have thermal covers.) An automatic cover on a pool dramatically reduces evaporation and therefore you're not sending

Btus into the atmosphere.

A couple years ago, we had a client who wanted to leave the pool open over the winter so she could use the attached spa. We studied the situation and found that the energy saved by her auto cover actually offset the cost of winterizing the pool, and she had use of the spa year-round.

Along with reduced evaporation, an auto cover contains any smell of chemicals that might be emanating from the surface. That may not be all that important in an outdoor pool, but it sure makes a huge difference in an indoor pool space. Also, by reducing evaporation, as mentioned just above, the cover reduces humidity in an indoor environment, which in turn means less energy required to dehumidify the room where the pool is located.

One limitation of automatic pool covers is that for the most part, they require pools to be rectangular. There are ways to apply them to other shapes, but that can be prohibitively expensive, which does pose a problem for some clients who really want a free-form pool with a creative shape. Fortunately, rectangular pools are beautiful in their simplicity and can fit in with almost any architectural style.

Yes, covers do add to the initial cost of the pool and there are far less expensive options. But as is true of other value-added features, the long-term savings and convenience, not to mention peace of mind, offered by an automatic cover makes it a feature well worth serious consideration.

Into the Bunker

Designing and building aquatic environments is always a matter of balancing aesthetics and function. Part of that challenge is simply deciding where to place the equipment.

Fact is, equipment is not pleasing to the eye with all the pipes, valves, conduits, and industrial-looking components. Unless you're fond of the appearance of machinery, equipment sets are unsightly and probably always will be. It's like the backstage in a theater, it's where the show really happens, but also the part that should always be hidden from view.

Equipment should also not be heard. The noise of pumps and other components can be as aesthetically invasive as an equipment set that's left in plain view. It can become a source of frequent annoyance to homeowners and sometimes their neighbors. Even with variable speed pump technology, which does significantly reduce noise, completely isolating outdoor living areas sonically will inevitably be a huge benefit for homeowners throughout the life of the pool.

These are the two primary reasons that whenever possible, I prefer to install equipment below grade in vaults, or as I like to call them, "bunkers." Yes, it adds cost to the project, but the gains in noise elimination, visual harmony, as well as making the most efficient use of space, all add up to a wise investment for the homeowner.

But there's more to it than just sight and sound. The value of real estate is another factor that pushes our clients and us in the downward direction. As housing prices increase and lot sizes shrink, there's a growing need to make the most out of all available space. If you calculate the cost per square foot of the area needed for a typical equipment set, especially one that's spread out enough for convenient service and repair, the value of that square footage can be considerable.

Added to that is the growing trend toward outdoor living. Many clients want to do more outside in terms of cooking, dining, and entertaining. That too can elevate the need to be as space efficient as possible. Again, going underground with the equipment is the perfect solution because it essentially expands the area you have available.

Finally, an equipment bunker provides the ultimate protection from the elements. The effects of weather, especially in our sometimes-harsh winters and searing hot summers, as well as the impact of UV degradation on equipment and plumbing, will almost inevitably shorten the life of the equipment. Plus, everything stays clean, which makes service easier, more pleasant and far more manageable.

Going Deep

There are, of course, different ways to go about locating an equipment bunker, which is largely dependent on the site specifics of the project at hand. Some builders opt for pre-manufactured, composite vaults that are installed somewhere adjacent to the pool below grade. There are hillside projects where cantilevered decks and pool structures can create spaces for locating equipment out of site and out of mind.

When possible, we take the concept a step further and actually locate the bunker below the pool shell itself, as described previously. We've taken this approach before and it works great. It gives us plenty of room to create a comfortable and accessible space, typically 10-by-20 feet with a seven-foot-high ceiling.

We build our bunkers out of reinforced poured-in-place concrete walls and floors, and of course with heavily reinforced ceilings. The structures are always engineered and built for the soil conditions, which in certain areas, means building for freeze-thaw conditions. We install adequate drainage, in case of equipment leaks and sealed penetrations for plumbing and heater ventilation. We also properly ventilate the space itself; and we install proper lighting and watertight doors.

We've built vaults with ladders and hatches, but when we can, we prefer to install steps and doors. Reason being, we want the equipment as accessible as possible so that homeowners and future servicers won't hesitate to enter the space and spend time there servicing the system.

Yes, installing equipment in bunkers does add cost to the project, considerable cost, sometimes as much as $40,000. Obviously, that number can dissuade some homeowners from the concept, but by the same token, for many in the high-end, custom category, it takes little or no convincing. They don't want to see or hear the equipment, and the additional advantage of saving space and protecting equipment also holds strong appeal.

Certainly, bunkers aren't for every project, but in the right situations, they offer an increased level of both enjoyment and product performance. That's why going below ground enhances the experience that takes place above.

Advancing Like Minds

Back above ground, when you're on a crusade, it's great to know that you're not alone.

That was the overwhelming feeling I had when I had the pleasure of attending the Water Quality Association's (WQA) 2018 Convention and Exposition in Denver. The event drew more than 3,000 professionals from a variety of industries, all with the shared interest of advancing water-treatment processes, techniques, and technology.

Being completely candid, sometimes here within the relatively narrow confines of the pool, spa, and aquatics recreation industry, it can get a little bit lonely as I and a relatively small cadre of other like-minded souls work to advance how we treat water and serve the public. I'm not complaining by any means, it's just that it can start to feel a bit like Sisyphus pushing the proverbial boulder up the hill.

One of my ongoing frustrations with the pool and spa

world is that, by and large, it has remained somewhat isolated from other water treatment industries. I truly believe that if more people from our industry attended these types of events and learned more about the WQA, the benefits of reaching beyond our self-imposed intellectual borders would be obvious.

What I found in Denver was therefore truly refreshing: a large number of kindred spirits from a spectrum of water-related camps all coming together to share information and collectively advance the cause for greater water quality. There were pros from public utilities, medicine, food processing, manufacturing, academia, research and development, and basically any type of endeavor where water quality is a pivotal concern.

The event's theme was "Elevation," which perfectly encapsulates the momentum and force behind what I personally see as a dramatic technical evolution. "This theme really speaks to the goal of the convention," said WQA Executive Director Pauli Undesser. "We believe our members are poised to elevate their businesses, their level of expertise, and their contribution to the betterment of water quality throughout the world."

Providing potable water to people in regions impacted by shortages, drought, and lack of infrastructure was one of the overriding themes at the event. So was overcoming important issues such as lead contamination, which affects hundreds of thousands, if not millions, of people in industrialized nations, especially here in the U.S.

The event was rich with discussions of technical advancements, such as LED-driven UV generation, improvement in reverse osmosis filtration, and nano-filtration media. There were sessions on different types of contamination and how to promulgate awareness of water quality issues throughout the public at large.

I came away from the event more convinced than ever that we have everything to gain by seeking out professionals from the greater world of water treatment, and really nothing to lose. By broadening our professional and intellectual associations, we might just find solutions and methods we hadn't previously considered.

A Kid's Eye View

Earlier I talked about how important and useful it is to listen to what people using a particular pool or spa say about their experience in the water. If they're complaining about the smell, or if their eyes are burning and they're having trouble breathing, those are strong indications that you need to take a hard look at the water conditions.

Experience has taught me that some of the most effective critics of water conditions are kids. They don't have adult filters yet and quite often cut right to the heart of the matter. In fact, I believe that if you talk to kids who enjoy swimming about their experience (there's that word again), their thoughts can instruct and influence the way we adults regard the importance of maintaining superior water quality.

Straight from the Source

Case in point, my 12-year-old daughter, Georgia, is one of those young people who was born with a keen knack for getting right to the point. She's also an experienced swimmer, including participation in a junior lifeguard program over the last two years.

We recently had a discussion about her thoughts on swimming and as is so often the case, she impressed her old dad with some rather sharp insights. "My favorite part of swimming is being able to float through the water," she said. "It feels like I'm flying. I feel like I can let out everything when I'm swimming. My least favorite part is when I have to get out of the water."

To that she added, "I like it when you can open your eyes underwater and it doesn't burn. Sometimes when you're in a saltwater or chlorine pool, it does burn and I just want to get out."

She expanded on that point by explaining that's why she prefers outdoor pools: "Because when you get out, the air is fresh. With indoor pools, when you get out, there's the chlorine smell and the room gets steamy. I don't swim much in the winter because there aren't indoor pools that don't have that chlorine smell. So, I look forward to summer because I can start swimming again. But it's critical that the water is clean and does not smell, otherwise I won't swim in it."

The Key Difference

Aside from my understandable parental pride, Georgia's "critical" remarks struck me in a surprisingly profound way from a professional perspective. As she explained, swimming is one of her favorite activities; she looks forward to it all winter and enjoys it so much that the worst part is having to stop. If that doesn't sound like the makings of a lifelong swimmer and possible future pool owner, I don't know what does.

However, she is equally adamant that if the water quality doesn't meet her expectations (that is, the water doesn't smell or burn her eyes), she doesn't even want to go near it in the first place. In other words, the condition of the water spells the difference between her favorite activity and one that she'd rather avoid. When we think about the bather experience, especially where kids are concerned, I firmly believe it's useful to remember that as professionals we have a choice whether or not we're helping to create aquatic enthusiasts or those who would rather stay away.

We should never lose sight of the fact that tomorrow's swimmers and pool owners are with us today.

My kids on the beach: Liam, Carlee, and Georgia

The Value of Superior Water Quality

Recently, a prospective client asked a very telling question. We were discussing the benefits of using our system, when the client asked, "What is the return on investment for our system as compared to using traditional chlorine-only sanitation?"

It certainly wasn't the first time I've been asked that question, and while I do understand why people want to know the ROI, especially given the upfront expense of our systems, it reveals a lack of understanding of the key issues they're facing in their own facilities.

For starters, it strikes me as misguided, even ironic, to compare doing something correctly to doing it the wrong way. It's like comparing the value of driving a high-performance automobile with state-of-the-art safety technology to the "affordability" of riding in a rusted jalopy with no doors, bald tires, and no brakes. All it takes is one accident and there really is no comparison.

When considering the ROI for our water-treatment system,

you have to take into account the cost of the problems that will be avoided by using the right set of treatment technologies. After all, establishing how quickly the system pays for itself goes far beyond simply defining how much will be saved by reducing chlorine use.

Questions of Cost

An accurate ROI calculation means asking a number of key questions, all of which lead to some sobering answers. Those queries should include:

How much revenue is lost during facility downtime due to water quality issues?

Quite simply, when the pool is closed for a day, a week, or longer, how much income do you lose? For high-use facilities, such as a resort or a competition pool, the numbers can get big in a hurry. That's especially true when considering ancillary revenue streams such as concessions, equipment rentals and premium offerings such as cabana rentals or fine dining.

Far more troubling and difficult to estimate, you have to ask:

What's the cost of having customers get sick from using your facility?

Leaving the possibility of a lawsuit and skyrocketing insurance premiums aside, disease outbreaks can be crushingly expensive, both in terms of dollars and public goodwill. Not only will the health department likely close the pool and possibly demand system upgrades, people who get sick from the water will almost certainly stop their patronage. They are also very likely to spread the word to family and friends that the facility should be avoided.

Beyond those two all-encompassing issues, even the more mundane concerns can result in huge costs.

What's the cost of draining and refilling the pool to correct water quality problems?

Some health departments require draining and refilling whether there are problems or not, but when there is an outbreak or other health issue of some kind, you can bet the health officials will require draining and refilling as part of the required remediation.

What's the cost of losing lifeguard and maintenance staff due to respiratory problems resulting from breathing chloramine-laden air?

There's already a shortage of lifeguards in many areas, and hiring and training new staff can be costly. Air and water quality will inevitably impact employee turnover and absenteeism.

The list goes on:

What's the cost of re-heating the pool or spa after it's been closed?

What's the cost of adding stopgap specialty chemicals such as clarifiers, algaecides, flocculants, and shock treatments in a constant effort to stay ahead of the water quality issues?

What's the cost of materials in and around the pool corroding?

It's well known that many indoor aquatic facilities in particular often undergo expensive renovations because they've been damaged by corrosion due to water and air-quality problems. In some cases, the costs of those types of repairs are so great the facilities are abandoned altogether.

And the most troubling question of all: *What's the cost of a bad public reputation?*

I'll leave that one to your imagination.

When you estimate and add up all of those factors, all of which are disturbingly common to pools treated by the antiquated chlorine-only method, you don't have to be an accountant to know that the risks of refusing to improve can be devastating. And that's true for everyone involved, from property owners, to management, to staff and especially to the consuming public.

Potential Values

Then there's the other side of the equation: how much do you stand to gain by way of maintaining truly gourmet water quality? (After all, the greater the gains, the greater the ROI.)

For example, when parents know that the environment is safe, wholesome, and enjoyable, they are far more apt to bring their kids there for fun, swim instruction, or even athletic training. I know from personal experience that as a parent when you can trust someone with your kids' well-being, you'll go out of your way to take advantage of those products, services, organizations, or facilities.

Likewise, when senior citizens are comfortable and confident in the water conditions and cleanliness of the facility, they too are more prone to use programs designed for their needs. The same is true for therapists and doctors who believe aquatic therapy and exercise will benefit their patients. Or coaches working with elite athletes — or basically anyone who loves the idea of being in the water but doesn't appreciate being exposed to possible health hazards.

All of this is why I believe the simple question, "What's the ROI for your system?" shows how much more work our industry must do to inform the public about water quality issues. We have everything to gain by pointing out the risks and costs but more important still, the benefits that attend making the best water treatment choices.

Yes, progress comes at a price, but we have to ask, what's the cost of refusing to change?

Fighting the Fear of Infection

In my opening query about whether or not pools have become obsolete, I mentioned how problems associated with pools have become cyclical narratives. Every year, for at least the last three years running, the U.S. Centers for Disease Control and Prevention (CDC) has released information about the spread of waterborne illnesses through contaminated water in pools, spas, and splash pads. The reports mainly focus on the risk of infection from *Cryptosporidium* and other pathogens. The information is then picked up by scores of news outlets across the country and often run with sensational headlines about "poop in pools."

It's scary, disgusting, and this year has been no exception. As an example, on May 17, 2018, CBS News released a chilling report on its website:

A new report from the Centers for Disease Control and Prevention (CDC) finds that a third of the outbreaks over a 14-year period occurred at hotel swimming pools. The report, published in CDC's Morbidity and Mortality Weekly Report, looked at data from 2000 through 2014 and found that 493 outbreaks were reported, resulting in at least 27,219 illnesses and eight deaths.

Cryptosporidium, also known as "crypto," a parasite tough enough to survive even in properly maintained pools, was the most common cause of illness. Crypto was responsible for 58 percent of outbreaks, and 89 percent of all illnesses, where a germ was identified and linked to pools, hot tubs and water playgrounds.

As is common for these types of news reports, it goes on to list preventive measures that will help keep crypto out of the water in the first place. Those recommendations include:

- Don't swim or let your kids swim if sick with diarrhea. If crypto is the cause of the diarrhea, wait until 2 weeks after diarrhea has stopped to go swimming.
- Don't swallow pool water.
- Take kids on bathroom breaks hourly, and change diapers in a diaper-changing area away from the water.
- Before swimming, check the facility's inspection score. Use a test strip from your local retailer or pool supply store to check if the water's pH and bromine or free chlorine levels are correct before getting in the water.

There's no doubt those recommendations if followed by the bathing public will help, although I do find it a stretch to imagine parents toting their own test strips poolside to check for pH and sanitizer levels. The problem is that all it takes is one infected person in the water to result in scores of infections. It's also worth noting that testing for crypto takes 10 to 14 days and costs $350 per test. In most, or all, cases, the presence of crypto is only known after someone gets sick.

The far more powerful bottom line is that we should be working together across the board to present the true solution, the ability to sanitize chlorine-resistant pathogens before someone becomes ill.

Relieving Concerns

All parents worry about their kids, it's what we do. I fret every day over every aspect of my three kids' lives. So much so, I've grown to accept that worry as a kind of life sentence, the price we pay for the greatest love we'll ever experience.

In fact, my impassioned journey into water quality management has been largely driven by parental concerns, my own and those of other dads and moms everywhere. While I've always been focused on health and safety, those worries in and around the water came to fruition when my kids got sick using a public swimming pool and suffered some rather serious respiratory conditions.

Suffice it to say that this dad was not a happy camper. It happened in a public pool where the treatment system, or lack thereof, was completely inadequate for the large bather load. The water smelled, it looked funky, and many of the lifeguards and swimmers brought inhalers with them. It was a completely unacceptable situation. Worse yet because swimming was part of my kid's school curriculum, we didn't have a choice of where to swim.

In addition to the common bummer that is caring for sick children, my experience building and servicing pools and spas had already long taught me that reliable, safe water is not only attainable, it's also essential. I kept thinking, we know how to do this and this is why! Seeing my own children needlessly compromised by pool water — my own industry — was far more than I could abide. Ever since, I've been a crusader for the profession of water quality management.

Worries Be Gone

The way I see it, parents have their plates piled high enough with anxiety. None need the added stress of worrying about their precious cargo getting damaged because the staff maintaining a community pool have no clue what they're doing. As an industry, we have a professional and, dare I say, a moral responsibility to make sure those worries do not come to pass, ever!

That profound sense of responsibility resides at the core of why I'm so passionate about water quality. We owe it to parents and their children who use recreational water to set those worries aside, and we owe it to ourselves to accept only perfect water quality — water that's properly sanitized, oxidized, filtered, and balanced, always without exception or excuse.

In purely pragmatic terms, we have a choice whether we engender a future generation of aquatic enthusiasts or turn them away. The enormous upside of this choice is that we do, indeed, have the wherewithal to alleviate parental concerns. That potential is within our collective grasp. The technology exists, the expertise exists and, for many, the desire exists. The only thing missing is the collective force, the professional mandate, to embrace the prime importance of making water quality, and the peace of mind it delivers, our top professional priority.

I've seen it work time and time again. I've seen how parents appreciate knowing the water their kids are immersed in, sometimes for hours at a time, is safe, wholesome, and assured. That level of trust and appreciation can only be developed over time and only by way of repeated experience. But when we do earn that trust, the extraordinary results can't be counted, only felt.

In place of the anxiety of worrying that our children are being exposed to unhealthy conditions, we can provide a wholesome and reliable environment that is not only free of concern but also filled with joy and good health. That's not too much to ask, and it's time our industry embraces that responsibility.

Safety Always

Whether in a swimming pool, the ocean, or even a bathtub, immersing your body in water always comes with an inherent set of risks. In swimming pools, those risks include not only drowning but also diving accidents, suction entrapment, slipping and falling, electrical shock, and waterborne illnesses. That's quite a list and unfortunately, every year far too many people fall prey to accidents in each of those categories.

In defining and promoting the role of the water quality manager, it's incumbent upon us to consider how to address water-related safety issues. Each of these risks comes with a specific profile of how and why accidents occur. We know that so long as people enter water incidents are inevitable. That does not mean, however, that there is any such thing as an acceptable number. As the cliché goes, one person getting hurt or worse is too many.

Child drowning clearly tops the litany of aquatic tragedies.

According to the Consumer Product Safety Commission, 350 children under the age of five drown in pools each year in the U.S. Combating that startling toll requires a multi-faceted approach that includes a combination of safety barriers (fences, safety covers, self-latching doors, and gates), the possible use of alarm systems, and most important of all, parental supervision. Safety advocates always point to layers of protection as the way to prevent child drowning.

Good Lessons

Swimming lessons also play an important part. While it is true that teaching kids to swim does not make them "drown proof" it does reduce the risk. The Centers for Disease Control and Prevention reports that participation in formal swimming lessons can reduce the risk of drowning by as much as 88 percent among children age one-to-four, those at the greatest risk of drowning. The American Academy of Pediatrics supports swimming lessons as young as age one.

Swimming lessons not only teach kids how to float safely and swim, they also engender good aquatic habits. It's important, for example, to teach kids to not swallow water as much as possible to avoid unnecessary exposure to infection. That goes hand in hand with also teaching the importance of regular bathroom breaks and a brief rinse in the shower before they get in the water. Sometimes safety comes down to the small things as well as the more obvious issues.

I believe it is up to every person involved in the aquatics world, from facility managers to pool builders to service technicians to lifeguards, swim instructors, and coaches — as well as parents —

to embrace and avidly promote these measures.

One way that the WQM can do the most good in his or her specific role is to prevent water quality problems that might forestall participation in swimming programs, as well as swimming at home. It's common sense: if people stay away from swim instruction because they've had bad experiences with poor water quality, they are at greater risk should they at some point decide to go swimming. Instruction in swimming and water safety makes everyone involved more aware of the risks, how to safely behave in water, and that can spell the difference between safety and catastrophe in almost any type of aquatic setting.

And, I believe everyone in all walks of life should be taught CPR.

The key to success in promoting safety ultimately is to not shy away from the issue, but instead to work to empower consumers with information and measures they need to protect their children and themselves. Practical information is both the anecdote to fear and the key to success.

This applies not only to child drowning prevention, but also to all of the other forms of risk in pools and spas. If, for example, we want to dispel the fear and eliminate the risk of suction entrapment, we should explain to consumers that all pools new and old should follow standards set by the Virginia Graeme Baker legislation. Things like split main drains and proper flow rates virtually eliminate the chance of an accident.

If a pool is meant for diving, it should be an adequate depth and have proper depth markers. If you know a pool is going to have heavy foot traffic on the deck, it should have a non-slip surface and no running signs. All pools must comply with the National Electric Codes and, of course, the water should always be kept free of pathogens and disinfection by-products.

It's encouraging to realize that all of the risks inherent in aquatic environments can be mitigated. The first step is acknowledging those risks and then after that, we all must actively promote safety measures, but not from a standpoint of fear. Instead we should attack the problem with confidence knowing that by working together and sharing information, we can protect ourselves, our families and everyone else.

Sensitive Perception

It's one of the truly unfortunate traits of human nature — we tend to ignore what we cannot see. We're an extremely visual species, and when something is invisible, there's a strong tendency for us to think that it's simply not there. What disturbs me the most about this characteristic is that it's true even when the unseen negatively impacts us, directly or indirectly.

Water quality is the perfect example. Water is, by nature, colorless and translucent. The vast majority of people only know whether it sparkles, tastes fresh, and doesn't smell bad. Beyond that, all the stuff about pH, pathogens, sanitizing methods, calcium hardness, total dissolved solids, disinfection by-products, metals, and dozens of other factors are completely obscure to most people.

Even when water does look funky and smells weird, many of us just ignore it and assume it's safe — until it bites us with some type of ailment, or worse. Because water is so ubiquitous, it is also easy to take it for granted, especially in societies where we have mostly adequate treatment systems. We live our lives in ignorant bliss. Potable water comes out the tap and the waste water goes down the drain.

On an Enormous Scale

One of the biggest examples of this out-of-sight-out-of-mind mentality is known as the Great Pacific Garbage Patch. Most people are completely unaware that between the West Coast of North America and Hawaii, there's a "patch" of garbage in the middle of the ocean that is, no kidding, twice the size of Texas. It's an expanse of mostly plastic trash that is pushed together by currents and now is larger than the vast majority of nations on the planet. And, it's killing fish and other essential marine life at an astonishing rate.

I don't mean to get on a soapbox here, but how can something that patently awful be allowed to happen? The basic answer is simple: we don't see it, and so most of us really and truly just don't care.

Another oceanic travesty is the rapidly dropping pH levels in ocean water around the globe. It's basic science, there's more carbon dioxide in the atmosphere than there used to be, and as a result, much of it gets absorbed in water, which becomes carbonic acid that in turn lowers the pH. Again, we don't see it, but it is evident in the destruction of coral reefs and critical species of plankton and krill, all of which leads to the collapse of entire marine ecosystems.

And, finally there are the dead zones that have grown at the mouths of major rivers. Compounds such as those containing ammonia and phosphates, common in fertilizer and pesticides, flow into rivers, and in turn, engender the growth of invasive algae species, which remove dissolved oxygen for the water as they decompose.

The results are vast areas where entire oceanic ecosystems disappear.

Closer to Home

What does any of this have to do with pools and spas, the primary focus of these discussions? The answer is *everything* because the problems we have with recreational water quality are at the most basic level due to the same lack of concern. We simply fail to pay attention to the conditions of the water.

In the case of pollution impacting natural waters, the problem is global in scale, but when we swim in pools that are contaminated or at least plagued with bad water chemistry, the issue becomes far more personal. Getting sick from bad water at the neighborhood pool may be miniscule by comparison, but it doesn't feel that way when you're the one or it's your kids who get sick. When a health department shuts down a commercial pool and costs the owners money, only then do those impacted start to consider the consequences of ignoring water quality, or doing the bare minimum required by codes.

Whether it's the oceans or the 500 gallons of water in your personal hot tub, we'd all do well to simply pay more attention and, dare I say, take action when we are confronted with unhealthy water. Better yet still, I imagine a world where we prevent problems before they get out of hand. Our lives depend on potable water, our health relies on people who know how to care for water, and, indeed, the entire life on our planet cannot sustain itself when it exists in what amounts to sewage.

We have to do better and we can do better. Perhaps if we start small and pay greater attention to water at the tap and the water we use for fun, relaxation, and wellness, maybe then our collective attention might shift to the much bigger pictures. But that all starts with a shift in mentality where we come to more fully appreciate the critical nature of healthy water where we choose to perceive more intently and deeply. Until we change the fundamental way we regard and value "aquatic hygiene," we are destined to fall prey to our own neglect.

Next time you drink a glass of clear, refreshing water or take a dip in a sparkling pool or inviting hot tub, think about all those elusive factors that impact water quality and how those unseen elements will affect your health. Yes, the pursuit of superior water quality is an idealistic journey, but it's also the ultimate practical concern. I believe we owe it to ourselves, each other, and the planet to look beyond that which immediately meets the eye.

Value and Price

One of the biggest obstacles standing in the way of widespread acceptance of advanced treatment technology, and indeed the entire approach to water quality management espoused in these discussions . . . is price.

It's a familiar refrain heard for as long as I can remember in this industry, and many other types of businesses, as well: too many property owners and managers are focused purely on the price tag and nothing else. Never mind quality. Never mind reputation. Never mind commitment to the end results and certainly never mind building relationships. No, these "transactional buyers" are all about price and price only. They will reflexively dismiss bids that are higher than others and often they are not entirely courteous in doing so.

By contrast, there are also buyers, albeit far fewer in numbers, who do value relationships based on reputation, vision, responsiveness, and sensitivity to their needs. And, above all they are also smart enough to see the long-term benefits of artisan water management. These clients understand simple things like clear water is not necessarily safe water and that it's better to prevent problems like infectious outbreaks, smelly water, algae blooms, and the build-up of disinfection by-products before they happen. They are predisposed to think that genuine value usually does not come at bargain-basement prices.

Fact is, anytime someone is working in a reactive mode to water problems, they've already lost the first battle and are fighting a rear-guard action. That's why we urge both our construction clients and our service customers to invest in systems and regimens that stave off trouble before it happens. After all, once you find yourself in the reactive mode of adding chemicals to correct issues, it becomes a kind of cat and mouse game of chasing the chemistry, and often never really stabilizing the situation.

Servicing an inadequately treated pool, one with inferior technology and non-expert service, will always be a compromise. Homeowners will become frustrated and even angry and in the case of the commercial facilities, the downtime and other issues stemming from water quality problems can become surprisingly costly, both in revenue and reputation.

A Clear Explanation

In our business, I have a saying that I'd rather explain my price than apologize for our service. No, we are never going to be the least expensive option, at least not up-front, but when you cast out the costs associated with water quality problems over one, two, five or ten years, it's abundantly easy to see that investing in our approach will pay for itself many, many times over. And, even more important, the life of the body of water will be defined by reliable operation, constant enjoyment, sound health and most important, biological safety.

The problem from our perspective is that there's no quick way to make that case and the transactional buyer doesn't want to hear it in the first place. Until a problem occurs, it's fair to say that water quality management is invisible to most people. When it's working, you don't really notice the water treatment system because a well-maintained body of water is simply there to enjoy without concern or worry.

As a result, it's easy to ignore, until it's too late.

All of that said, when clients step beyond the reactive and transactional mindset, it's amazing how satisfied they become, especially over the long haul. Pools and spas can represent massive investments and they become daily parts of people's lives. Our more mindful, relationship-driven clients quickly realize and appreciate that the money they've spent on our system and our service yields benefits they can enjoy every day and that over the long haul, they do, in point of fact, save money.

That's why even though it can be tremendously frustrating when being beat up about the head and shoulders over price, we never give up. We know through years of experience both building and servicing pools and spas, that we are offering far greater value than some of our competitors that are looking to shave off small margins of profit by selling down-and-dirty service and systems of inferior engineering and construction.

Never Giving Up

It's not an easy sell, because to some degree most people are rightfully concerned about how much money they spend and many take that concern to the point of obsession, but for those who do consider the broader more long-term implications and benefits of our approach to artisan water quality management, the results always speak for themselves, in terms of dollars and otherwise.

We know there are always going to be those customers who will opt for the cheaper options. And, we also know there will always be those companies in our industry that themselves are lock-step with the transactional approach to doing business and rely on cheap price tags to rope in unsuspecting customers. Our goal and our approach, by stark contrast, has always been to tip the margins toward quality; to make the case that investing in water quality is akin to investing in a quality car or a beautiful home.

Consider the fact that for the average homeowner, or commercial property owner for that matter, the aquatic environment often represents the second biggest investment they ever make behind their home or facility itself. Given the enormity of the financial commitment, I ask is that really where you want to skimp on quality? A poorly built house might be marginally less expensive in the short run, but is there any question that corners cut by the builder will come back to haunt the buyer with frustration and expense down the line?

The old adage is true: you do get what you pay for. Focusing purely on price is essentially a sure-fire way to ensure added expense down the line as well as the disillusionment that comes with substandard operation and water conditions.

It's ironic, I suppose, that the cheapest options are ultimately almost always really and truly the most costly.

Beneath the Surface

Water may be the most wonderful and amazing of natural elements, and it can be one of the most destructive. From its ability to carve the Grand Canyon to the slow rot that occurs when water finds its way into the walls of your home, you can never underestimate the damage it can do.

Even in swimming pools, structures that are by their very nature designed to contain and control it, water will often slowly deteriorate both cosmetic and structural elements. And if it's not stopped, it can slowly destroy the entire vessel.

Case in point, every year in spring, we pull scores of winterizing covers off of pools as we open them for summer. When we do, we find many instances where tiles have popped off the waterline and pieces of coping that have separated from the bond beam substrate. This happens because of the freeze-thaw cycles that occur over winter, where the ground expands and contracts because of the freezing and thawing of groundwater that surrounds the pool structure. It's an extremely common issue that will happen to almost every pool at some point.

Most of the time, it's a relatively minor repair that can be easily handled over the course of the summer. The big problems start, however, when homeowners decline to address the issue before the following winter.

Cyclical Damage

What happens is the damage caused by freeze-thaw cycles creates places in the form of small cracks and fissures where water can enter the pool structure. It slowly seeps behind the surface and spreads by way of its wicking action. Concrete is full of tiny voids, and when the surface that contains water in the pool is compromised, water will get in the structure and will start to spread.

That liquid intrusion in turn leads to deterioration of the concrete shell and its structural steel. If left unchecked, entire walls of the pool will basically turn to sand and the still will rust into nothing. It's similar to what happens when you get a cavity in a tooth. The chemistry in your mouth slowly but surely spreads and if you don't repair the cavity with a filling, you lose the entire tooth.

In pools, water can intrude from not only the inside of the pool, but also from the ground that surrounds it. This dual threat will not only exacerbate the damage caused by freeze-thaw cycles, it also worsens the spread of the concrete deterioration. It all adds up to a nasty domino effect that will eventually destroy your pool structure. All of that is why it is so important to correct these issues while they're in the early stages. If you don't, what starts as an extremely minor repair will, over time, turn into one that can require demolishing large portions of your pool's structure. When left unattended over years, you might even need to remove the entire pool shell.

That is why we always recommend taking those falling tiles and loose copingstones right away. Have a repair company come in and not only replace the tile and coping, but also remove damaged concrete and apply waterproofing agents as needed.

And, if you're in the process of building a new pool, be sure to talk to your contractor about using waterproofing products to slow the inevitable march of water's destructive power.

When it comes to water's ability to damage concrete structure, or any structure for that matter, don't wait until the problem becomes catastrophic, because eventually, it will.

The interior surface is a swimming pool's largest and most important aesthetic feature. Surfaces are responsible for the pool's appearance and also for bather comfort. A "healthy" surface will give you years of visual enjoyment and tactile pleasure when you're in the water, and on top of that, it helps the pool remain watertight.

Whether it's an exposed aggregate surface, white or colored plaster or even tile, we ask a lot of the material that lines our pools. Pool surfaces are made to withstand the rigors of constant exposure to water, the universal solvent, and the wear and tear that comes with use. That's a big part of why water's mineral balance and proper sanitation are so important, as well as routine cleaning.

A well-maintained pool will extend the life of the surface

while improper maintenance can dramatically shorten it. There are a number of problems that can afflict a surface, especially plaster. Common issues include metal staining, calcium scale, etching, mottling, and algae.

Ironically, in a plastered pool, by far the most common surface material, the chemical compound that makes the surface both smooth and beautiful is also the most susceptible to chemical degradation. It's called calcium hydroxide, which forms the "cream" coat, which makes the plaster surface smooth. It's a highly soluble compound when exposed to aggressive water chemistry and will deteriorate over time when constantly fluctuating chemical conditions.

This why it's so important to repair the surface once it starts to show signs of wear. Often, a degraded surface will not only look shabby with inconsistent color and stains, it can also become rough to the touch. When plaster goes bad, you'll feel a texture that's akin to sandpaper. When it gets bad enough, it can even cause minor abrasions and significant discomfort.

Also, when the cycle of decay sets in, the roughened surface becomes more porous and thus more susceptible to algae blooms and staining. It's a nasty domino effect that can transform a beautiful body of water into an eyesore.

As is true of other types of pool repairs, fixing the surface is a minor task when it's done early on, but if you leave the damaged areas untreated over a period of years, you could wind up with a hefty repair job that might involve removing the entire surface and replacing it, a costly undertaking that can run into the thousands.

Because interior surfaces are constantly exposed to water, it's close to inevitable that you will need some repair work at some point, but how extensive the repair depends almost entirely on when you have the work done. Yes, proper water chemistry and cleaning are big helps in forestalling repairs, but at some point, even the best maintained pool will need some surface work. It's the nature of structures that contain water.

When the work is minor, the cost is significantly less and the downtime in the pool will also be minimal. But when you let it go, the resurfacing process becomes messy and expensive.

Finding the Balance

I'd like to bring this ranging discussion back full circle to one of the key elements of water quality management, which I touched on briefly in the earlier chapter on running a service business.

Within the profession of water quality management, there are several subcategories of expertise needed in order to be effective. One of the most important is how to manage and maintain mineral balance in water. Mineral balance may be arguably the most fundamental aspect of managing water. In both tangible and conceptual ways, finding the balance is the challenge from which all others in this field begin.

When we talk about "balanced water," that means water that is in a state of equilibrium. All water contains minerals, chiefly calcium, but many others as well. When it's "balanced," that means it does not need to absorb more minerals nor does it need to release or "precipitate" them. It is, to borrow a phrase "at peace."

That sounds simple enough, but it's much more complicated. Reason being, everything in water chemistry is interrelated and there are places that mineral balance intersects with sanitization and other key areas. Yet, at the same time, it is very much also its own science.

Truth is, all of the facets of water chemistry hold hands; they all exist in a state of shifting balance. It's actually kind of a beautiful relationship, especially when everything is working. But when one part of the recipe is out of whack, it can cause a domino effect that ultimately compromises water quality and the user experience.

Mineral balance in particular directly impacts bather comfort, sanitizer and oxidizer efficiency, the texture and feel of the water, the appearance of interior surfaces (especially plaster), and the cost and effort required to maintain the pool. It encompasses the most basic set of pool and spa service cannons, the almighty litany of pH, total alkalinity, calcium hardness, total dissolved solids, and water temperature.

That's a lot to consider but fortunately we have long had the tools to successfully manage water balance. Testing products and technology are reliable, assuming you know how to use them, and we have a wonderful system for calculating the cumulative effect of the key chemical constituents.

Specifically, all of those values I listed just above together comprise the enduring Langelier Saturation Index (LSI), which has been used since the fifties to balance water across a range of applications. Originally developed for closed aquatic systems, i.e., those not exposed to the environment, such as public utility and industrial applications, the LSI was adapted to the open-air systems of pools, spas, and other types of decorative and recreational water features.

Technically speaking in the narrowest definition, it's an approximate measure of water's level of saturation of calcium carbonate. In the broader more directly applicable sense, it indicates whether water is aggressive, meaning it is deficient in minerals and will "seek" to balance itself by dissolving minerals, such as the calcium compounds in plaster. Or, conversely, how over-saturated water is with minerals causing calcium compounds and metals to precipitate out of solution in the form of scale or stains.

Without going into a formal primer on LSI calculations, information that's widely available in other resources, suffice to say maintaining the water as close to a zero value, which is perfectly balanced water, the more stable all aspects of your water chemistry will remain. Without a working understanding of how the values that factor into the LSI all work together, water management becomes nothing more than guesswork.

This is why in midsummer we recommend to our clients that we conduct a full chemistry index. This process gives us a comprehensive understanding of all the key chemical constituents in the water. Chief among those is the water balance, specifically calcium hardness and total alkalinity. We've learned that those two factors can be the toughest to keep up with. We like to see calcium at about 250 ppm but due to splash out it drops to down to about 150 to 180 ppm, then the alkalinity falls from about 120 ppm to 70 ppm, and that leads to pH fluctuations. Most of the time, you don't see the difference, the water still looks clear, but when the levels start to shift, we start hearing complaints about bather comfort and the water becomes much more difficult to manage. It's either going to be corrosive or scaling because the pH is fluctuating and constantly bouncing back and forth. It's amazing how the LSI is influenced by a relatively minor shift in pH.

The precise methods and chemicals used to manipulate levels vary among professionals. For example, we prefer using calcium chloride for raising calcium and food-grade sodium bicarbonate (Arm and Hammer granular #5) to raise total alkalinity. Although balance control is still largely done by hand for the vast majority of pools, there are automated systems for pH monitoring and adjustment. In those systems we use CO_2 to maintain pH at the perfect 7.5 level. As technology advances, there will be more and more opportunities to take the control of water balance out of human hands. That's a positive because as is the case with sanitizing and oxidizing, the more automated the system becomes, the more reliable and less likely to experience fluctuations.

It's also worth noting that when we reduce the chlorine compounds used, the less the influence on water balance. Again, it's all a subtle applied science that's crucial to the work of the water quality professional.

Why SRK?

A potential client recently asked me why he should choose our company. Frankly, I was surprised by my sudden inability to offer a concise answer. I muddled through the conversation, but later the exchange prompted me to consider the crux of the answer to his question.

As I was jotting down my thoughts, it dawned on me that the response to his query works as something of a professional manifesto for the profession of water quality management.

Here's what I came up with . . .

Because we are passionate about the Aquatic Experience

Because we've spent decades mastering the fine arts and crafts of water quality management

Because we apply the highest possible standards to all phases of design, engineering, construction, and service

Because we base our work on science, research, engineering, and the latest technology

Because we are also parents who understand the importance of wholesome, clean, sanitary, and inviting water quality

Because we understand that downtime is costly

Because we are dedicated to avoiding water quality issues that lead to pool closures

Because we work with all types of aquatic environments, from the simplest backyard pool to the most complex public aquatic center

Because we are always approachable and make a point of actively listening to your concerns and priorities

Because we tailor our work to your needs and best interests

Because we are constantly educating ourselves and improving all aspects of our work

Because we understand how decisions made during the design phase impact what happens throughout the life of the facility

Because we resolve problems quickly and effectively

Because we don't believe in short cuts and half measures

Because we do not compromise

Because of we believe in the future of the aquatic lifestyle

Because through the application of science and technology we can increase the value of aquatic participation

Because we are professionals of the most dedicated kind

Because we work only in verifiable information and never make false claims

Because we are the best at what we do

Because we are humbled by the opportunity to serve our clients and our communities

Because we value water

Because we love what we do

Epilogue

Painting in Water

I've always been amazed and delighted by how beauty can emerge from the unexpected, or even an accident. My life experiences working with and enjoying water have revealed countless epiphanies, large and small, a process of unexpected discovery the likes of which have driven the creative instincts of some of history's greatest artists, inventors, and philosophers.

One of the best examples I can think of was how the great modernist painter Jackson Pollock discovered his groundbreaking drip-painting technique when he spilled paint on the floor of his studio. That simple accident and resulting recognition on Pollock's part led to a revolution that shook the art world to its core, a sea change that is being felt to this day.

On an infinitely smaller scale, the same kind of thing happened to me about three years ago. And, like Pollock, my simple unexpected observation has led to a mode of making art that has become a significant and intensely enjoyable sideline to my career working as a water quality professional.

As I've perfected the art and craft of creating beautiful water, I've found myself falling more and more in love with the aesthetics of the aquatic experience. When water is crystal clear, polished, and inviting, it becomes one of the most beautiful design elements we experience anywhere. The way the light plays within the liquid matrix, the texture, random motion and infinite patterns, the reflective quality, the way water distorts size and depth, and how it influences the physical movements of people and animals—every aspect of it can be the source of unending wonderment. At least it is for me and I know for a lot of other people in different ways.

All of that is why I've always enjoyed sailing on the ocean. The sensory experiences of being on the water transport me to a different state of consciousness, as if traveling to a beautiful alien world. Recognizing the impact that water has on my senses, emotions, and awareness, I started spending more and more time sitting underwater and simply looking around.

I found that through the aperture of my mask, I was seeing the world aquatic in a whole new way. All of the amazing qualities I've always admired about water suddenly took on more dimensions and greater depth. No longer was water simply a beautiful reflective surface, which is amazing enough in and of itself, but submerged it becomes more visually prismatic, more all-encompassing.

It didn't take long before I started making digital videos of my little underwater excursions, which were mostly confined to my own backyard pool. Using a GoPro camera, I began capturing the temporal nature of the motion and the random spontaneity of the liquid space. By recording those magic moments, I was then able to go back and study the visual qualities more deliberately and in greater detail.

Along the way, I was struck by how varied and even abstract many of the images seemed to be. I started looking at each frame and began to see them as individual works of natural art. In those raw images, I started to see a different kind of aesthetic potential.

One day, just for fun, I took some of my favorite "stills" from the videos and loaded them into Photoshop, where I began to manipulate the colors, distort the shapes, play with saturation, sharpness, tint, and texture. Almost immediately, I found that with some creative manipulation, I could take those already beautiful images and make something that, to my eyes, looked and felt completely new.

It wasn't long before I was turning out piece after piece of what mostly looked like abstract art. Some of the images do still look like water, especially those where I've captured someone swimming, floating, or diving into the water. Other pieces take on a visual quality that are not directly identifiable as water, per se, but, to my eyes, always carry the spirit and mystery of the fluid matrix.

Over the past few years, I've started displaying these works in our show room and have even talked to people at different art galleries and art dealers in nearby New York City about someday showing and selling my pieces. Much to my delight, the feedback I've received has been incredibly positive, and now my modest random observations are turning into a potentially substantial personal and, even possibly professional, pursuit.

Eyes Wide Open

Now that I've found my own way to be involved in an artistic endeavor, I've come to realize that art really is the product of how we choose to look at the world, and then how we try to express what we see. When Pollock spilled the paint on his studio floor, it's likely that every other person on the planet would've just seen a small mess that needed to be cleaned. But Pollock instead saw spectrums of unexpressed creative possibility.

Although I would never compare myself to his level of genius, I do now see that kind of purely creative path far more clearly. When I look at the way water "paints" the world, I see so much more than I once did. It's the magic of the moment, the beauty of the accident, and the gift of the unexpected.

That's why I can't wait to see what "painting in water" will reveal next.

About the Author

Steve Kenny is an aquatic designer, builder, and service technician with more than 25 years of experience. Based in Long Island, New York, he specializes in designing, building, and maintaining commercial and residential pools and spas that feature the highest possible water quality.

He is a passionate advocate of creating a new class of aquatic professionals devoted to the science, methods, and art of ensuring pristine water conditions. Steve was formally trained in the culinary arts and has a passion for fine dining. He is an accomplished photographer and sailing enthusiast. He is also a passionate advocate of the benefits of hydrotherapy.

A devoted family man, Steve lives in East Hampton with his bride of 20 years and their three children.